Buzzing Hemisphere   Rumor Hemisférico

Camino del Sol
A Latina and Latino Literary Series

Buzzing Hemisphere

Rumor Hemisférico

Urayoán Noel

THE UNIVERSITY OF
ARIZONA PRESS

TUCSON

The University of Arizona Press
www.uapress.arizona.edu

Printed in the United States of America
20 19 18 17 16 15   6 5 4 3 2 1

ISBN-13: 978-0-8165-3168-4 (paper)

Cover designed by Leigh McDonald
Cover art: *delusion* by Martha Clippinger

Publication of this book is made possible in part by the proceeds of a permanent
endowment created with the assistance of a Challenge Grant from the National
Endowment for the Humanities, a federal agency.

Library of Congress Cataloging-in-Publication Data
Noel, Urayoán.
  Buzzing hemisphere = Rumor hemisférico / Urayoán Noel.
    pages cm. — (Camino del sol, a Latina and Latino literary series)
  Parallel title: Rumor hemisférico
    ISBN 978-0-8165-3168-4 (pbk. : alk. paper)
  1. Hispanic Americans—Poetry. I. Noel, Urayoán. Poems. English. Selections. II.
Noel, Urayoán. Poems. Spanish. Selections. III. Title. IV. Title: Rumor hemisférico.
V. Series: Camino del sol.
  PS3614.O39B89 2015
  811'.6—dc23
                                      2015001463

♾ This paper meets the requirements of ANSI/NISO Z39.48-1992 (Permanence of
Paper).

"We owe it, therefore, to candor and to the amicable relations existing between the United States and those powers to declare that we should consider any attempt on their part to extend their system to any portion of this hemisphere as dangerous to our peace and safety."

—James Monroe, President of the United States (1823)

"Acoustic and phonological phenomena are processed in different hemispheres of the brain, which becomes fully specialized around age twelve; while sounds are processed in the right hemisphere, speech is processed in the left. Poetic language must be processed both acoustically and phonologically, in both hemispheres, because it carries acoustic information in excess of the linguistic information. . . . In processing acoustic information, a 'universal' or shared history intersects with a personal and language-specific history, for the emotional associations of the sounds of words seem to be partly determined by the cognitive processes of speech recognition and hold across languages."

—Mutlu Konuk Blasing, *Lyric Poetry: The Pain and the Pleasure of Words* (2006)

CONTENTS

HEMISPHERES / HEMISFERIOS

BUZZ / RUMOR

HEMISPHERES

HEMISFERIOS

"We are, too, the others"

William Carlos Williams, *In the American Grain*

ALPHABET CITY

CIUDAD ALFABETO

Come down and die with me   as lacquer shades our lack   and people walk off
subways   limning the wound   our bodies   mere bodies   salivating syllables
no longer citizens of silence   now saluting side streets   sending salvos to missing
siblings   becoming city's augury   through distances   as rats cross sidewalks
like dark merchandise   or toxins seeping through the capital

anteayer **b**arullos
cumulonimbos **d**ecapitando **e**stas **f**acetas
graciosos **h**uyendo **i**nmigrando **j**untos
kilométrico **l**argo **m**aratón **n**atimuerto
ñoco **o**jo **p**odrido **q**uizás
resuelva **s**u **t**álamo
útil **v**iolencia
weekend **x**enófobo
yanquilandia **z**igzagueando

as **b**efore
cloudbursts **d**raping **e**very **f**eature
grimy **h**eaven's **i**mmigrant **j**oy
knotted **l**ong **m**etal **n**ooses
outcast **p**osses **q**uickly **r**ivaled
streaming **t**raitors
useful **v**iolence
weekend **x**enophobia
yankees **z**igzagging

Baja a morir conmigo   donde la laca oculta la carencia   y la gente sale de los trenes
bordeando la herida   nuestros cuerpos   apenas cuerpos   salivando sílabas   ya
no ciudadanos del silencio   ahora saludando callejones   invocando a hermanos
invisibles   volviéndonos augurio de ciudad   entre distancias   mientras las ratas
cruzan aceras   como oscura mercancía   o como las toxinas de la capital

Come down with me   it's midnight in the banking centers   and nothing is stirring
on the trade routes   nothing more than topsoil founds this prophecy   these
boulevards in shards   this untracked form   this memory of water   our planet
found dry   our birthright is a metal   with no foundry   a language unfounded
a web   a womb   a tombic zone   perhaps a road   a door ajar   a wordless
sermon   in the wireless morning   of the shared mire

así bastante cruel
disqueras exitosas fabricando guarachas
harapo isótopo jarra kiosco
latifundistas mercenarios
naciones ñangotadas
otro pastiche que reclama
su trópico usurpado
villorrios whatever
x-men yihadistas zombis

alas big cruelties
deejays everywhere freestyle gutters
haberdasher isotope jars
killjoy landlocked musicians
nursing outsized pastiches
quirk rally
sun tropics upended
village wreckage
x-men yes-men zombies

Baja conmigo   es medianoche en el distrito bancario   y ya nada se mueve en las
rutas comerciales   la profecía de trizas es pura polvareda   bulevares trizados
esta forma sin huella   esta memoria de agua   nuestro planeta a secas   nuestra
herencia de metal   infundible   un lenguaje no fundado   una red   un vientre
un lapidario   tal vez un camino   una puerta entreabierta   un sermón sin palabras
en la mañana inalámbrica   del lodo compartido

*Come down with me   skirting the sea   alone in airports   amid garbled
announcements   between the abyss and its voice-overs   the body and its torsions
the pulse in lesions   the memory that bludgeons   in televised tropics   full of
dark faces   signs of a present absence   awaiting landings and dreaming of family
bounded by breeze   nearing the beaches and observatories in lockdown*

acompáñenme **b**ucéfalos **c**omelibros
definitivamente **e**stoy **f**ebril
grandes **h**allazgos **i**ntuyo **j**adeando
kantianos **l**ameculos **m**alhaya
noticieros **ñ**apa **o**bligatoria
parecemos **q**uimeras **r**epitiendo **s**ecuestros
tecnócratas **u**rbanos **v**isitando **w**ikipedia
xenófobos **y**outubeando **z**ozobras

accomplished **b**ookworms **c**an
definitely **e**ntertain **f**everish **g**randeurs
huddled **i**n **j**izz-stained **k**nowledge **l**abs
many **n**ews **o**rphans **p**refer **q**uizzing
radically **s**ectarian **t**echnocrats
utterance **v**acancy **w**orkshops
xeroxed **y**outubed **z**ip-drived

*Baja conmigo   bordeando el mar   solos en aeropuertos   entre anuncios
indescifrables   entre el abismo y la voz doblada   el cuerpo y sus torsiones   el
pulso y sus lesiones   la memoria de sangre   en trópicos televisados   llenos de
caras oscuras   de señales de presencia en la ausencia   esperando aterrizajes y
soñando con familia   rodeados de brisa   acercándonos a observatorios y balnearios
clausurados*

The island and its buoys   the lone convoy   its shopping centers   and medical centers   and community and convention centers   because what's conventional is the idea of a center   the same one that could not hold   could not contain the continent   revealing the fixtures of a gutted landscape   fractures of sky

ancestros blogueros
caribeños diaspóricos
eróticos feos gagos herejes
intensidades junglas kamikazes
lampiños motines nórdicos
ñandús occipitales pichones quietecitos
relinchemos suavemente tumefactos universos
violentándote wachimán xto.
yo zambulléndome

ancestral bloggers
caribbean diasporas
erotic freeloaders gagging heresies
intense jungle kamikazes
language mutinies northbound
overly performative quietude
rhizomatic sweetheart texts
unite valiant workmates!
xmas yarmulke zone

La isla y sus boyas   su convoy solitario   sus centros comerciales y médicos   y comunales y de convenciones   porque es convencional la idea de un centro   el mismo que no aguanta   no contiene al continente   revelando los enseres en el paisaje arrasado   las fracturas de cielo

Come down with me   to sing in open vowels   because a poetics of gutting
would start at the limn   the lintel of the word   found and unfounded   in this
mainline sky   ripe for the staging   of a new terror

archipiélago
brillo **c**iego
delta **e**stuario
flujo **g**lobal
hemisferio **i**sla
jardín **k**ermés **l**abor
multitud **n**aciente
ñáñigo **o**ligarca
paraíso **q**uimérico
rascacielos **s**elva
tránsito **u**sual
vendaval
washington **x**ochimilco
ya **z**arpamos

archipelago
brilliant **c**ityscape
delta **e**stuary
flows **g**lobal
hemispheric **i**sland
jurisdiction **k**eypad
labor **m**ultitude
numbered **o**ligarchs
paradise **q**uicksand
razed **s**kyscraper **t**otems
underground **v**isions
washington **x**ochimilco
yesterday's **z**eitgeist

Baja conmigo   a entonar en vocales abiertas   porque una poética del ras   empezaría
por el trazo   el lintel de la palabra   hallada y no fundada   en este cielo
intravenoso   listo para el montaje   de un nuevo terror

Come down with me   in search of the city   and whatever it lets us share   already sick of the teachable moments   and the banking-crisis-recovery hymns   that leave us like pop-ups in the skyline   decoding the spyware on our skin   and yet we claim these endomorphic islands   alive in former factories of feeling   neglected but not yet disassembled

aquí **b**ebemos **c**erveza **d**esabrida
esperamos **f**amilia
gozamos **h**asta **i**nmolarnos **j**untos
karaoke **l**engüisucio
masticando **n**uestro **ñ**ame **o** **p**anapén
(¡**q**ué **r**ico **s**abe!
tragamos)
un **v**iejo **w**hitman **x**ilográfico
yace **z**arrapastroso

are **b**eer **c**ans **d**isposable?
every **f**amily **g**rows
hating **i**tself
joint **k**araoke **l**ives
mouthing **n**othing
our **p**reference?
queer **r**egret
silent **t**urmoil
undressing
viewing **w**hitman's **x**-film
yielding **z**ilch

Baja conmigo   en busca de la ciudad   y lo que nos deje compartir   hastiados ya de lecciones y elecciones   de las crisis bancarias con sus himnos redentores que nos dejan como virus en el horizonte   descifrando los programas espía en nuestra piel   y no obstante reclamamos estas islas endormorfas   vivos y coleando en las antiguas fábricas de afecto   pasados por alto   pero aún no desensamblados

*Come down with me   we will be together as children of trade   in the shadow of
slave ships   seeking out the parity of music   the death fugue in each other's eyes
in cities of migrants seeking asylum   in port cities where the silence is what ails
with their soil of rueful smiles   with the pain of crossing   with the marrow of
horizon and the echoes of coral   undulating in sunscape in borrowed skin   yet
warmed by blood currents*

anunciaban **b**andas
conciertos **d**esiertos
estadios **f**alsos
gran **h**azaña **i**mposible
jodido **k**arma
lóbrega **m**añana
nosotros **ñ**oños
o **p**eor **q**uitados
rindiéndonos **s**úbitamente
tontos **u**tópicos
velando **w**alkirias
xilófonos **y** **z**ampoñas

absent **b**ands
concerts **d**eserted
empty **f**ields
go **h**uman (**i**mpossibly)
jaded **k**arma
lousy **m**orning
noticing **o**urselves (**p**rovisionally)
quitters' **r**evolution (**s**orta)
tongued-tied **u**topian
valkyrie **w**atchers
xylophones
yowling **z**ithers

*Baja conmigo   nos veremos juntos como hijos del comercio   a la sombra de barcos
esclavistas   buscando la paridad de la música   la fuga en la mirada   en ciudades
migratorias sin asilo   en ciudades portuarias enfermas de silencio   pero rebosantes
de sonrisas tristes   con el dolor de cruzar   con la médula del horizonte y los ecos
de coral   ondulando bajo soles en una piel prestada   pero con el calorcito de
sangrientas corrientes*

For the sea   is what we sound like   from memory   imperfect of course   this
memory of empire   surrounded by shadows   by brown sands   in the half-life
of islands   affixed to the dark   against the beauty   at the edge of these lands
an assailed hemisphere   whose alleys gleam   like searchlights on a corpse

anómalas **b**estias
criaturas **d**esamarradas
escoria **f**eliz
gimiendo **h**asta **i**ncinerarse **j**ubilosamente
kerosén **l**ingüístico
matorral **n**euronal
ñu **o**rnitorrinco **p**ingüino
quinientos **r**ibosomas **s**omos
trapos **u**nicelulares
virus **w**hisky
xilema **y**erbajo **z**oo

anomalous **b**easts
creatures **d**reaming
effortlessly **f**ree
groaning **h**urt **i**n **j**ubilation's
knowing **l**ockstep
mired **n**eurons
oxen **p**latypuses **q**uasars
ribosomes **s**aplings
teeming **u**nicellular **v**iruses
wakeful **x**ylem
yearning **z**oo

El mar es cómo   nos hablamos de memoria   siempre imperfecta claro   la
memoria de imperios   de sombras a intemperie   de arenas oscuras   en la
media vida de islas   aferrados a tinieblas   ante la belleza de estas tierras   un
hemisferio asediado   cuyos callejones brillan   como reflectores sobre un cadáver

MI HEMISFERIO ARDIENTE

El cuatro de julio que pasé en el hospital me desperté frente a la cara manchada de los muelles al otro lado del East River. Esa noche los fuegos artificiales se arrastrarían por mi piel como serpientes, evocando la maraña de alambres en mi cráneo.

Mi epileptólogo me diría luego, tienes suerte (de ser poeta, quiso decir, y trabajar con la parte lingüística del cerebro, en la escuela, a mi propio ritmo—o al menos eso fue lo que entendí).

Tratando de sonar inteligente, asentí murmurando algo de que si neuronas y hemisferios dominantes, pero al fin fue la niebla la que me dominó. No era niebla de río, era la niebla del yo en su tránsito difícil, viendo entre ventanas sucias a las ciudades por fin festivas.

Él sencillamente pudiera haber dicho "es que el cielo no clarea por nadie" y yo quizás hubiera estado de acuerdo, si hubiera tenido la fuerza, si las serpientes no hubieran vuelto.

MY BURNING HEMISPHERE

The July fourth I spent at the hospital I woke up staring at the smudge of waterfront across the East River. That night the fireworks would crawl like serpents up my skin, matching the wires tangled in my head.

My epileptologist would later tell me, you're lucky (to be a poet, he meant, and work with the language part of the brain, in school, at my own pace—or at least that's how I heard it).

Trying to seem smart, I nodded, mumbling something about neurons and dominant hemispheres, but soon the fog had dominated me. It wasn't river fog, it was the fog of self as it slogs through way stations, looking out smudged windows at cities for once festive.

He might have simply said "the sky, it clears for no one," and I might have started to agree, had I had the strength, had the serpents not returned.

(2003)

MY BURNING HEMISPHERE

Irony is like the time I lost two front teeth, collapsing on the street outside the drugstore, too late for refills but just in time to fall.

I ended up at Saint Vincent's Hospital in a hallway where the sunlight flickered like synapses under strobes. Now the hospital is gone, and the newspaper reports on the clinics that replaced it.

Losing the muse, I find myself siding with the lost, a damaged beauty, a music I can't manage, no words for it in either of my native tongues, *rumor* in both.

I'm a mirror image of a hemisphere in shards, a hum that lumbers through the war zones, an axon, an aimless song calling the fire home.

MI HEMISFERIO ARDIENTE

La ironía es como cuando perdí los dos dientes de alante, desmayado en la calle frente a la farmacia, demasiado tarde para la receta pero justo a tiempo para la caída.

Acabé por fin en el hospital Saint Vincent, en un pasillo cuyos destellos de sol eran como sinapsis estroboscópicas. Ahora el hospital ya no está, y los diarios describen las clínicas que han tomado su lugar.

Extraviada la musa, me hallo del lado de los perdidos, una belleza averiada, una música que no manejo, pues me faltan las palabras en mis dos lenguas nativas, *rumor* en ambas.

Soy el reflejo de un hemisferio hecho trizas, un zumbido que se arrastra entre zonas de guerra, un axón, un cantar sin rumbo, llamándole hogar a las llamas.

(2007)

VOZ QUEBRADA

poema oral improvisado en un smartphone
Cripple Creek, Tallahassee, Florida, 2009

> "Todo
> duerme aquí sofocado
> bajo la línea muerta que recorta
> el ras rígido y firme de los campos"

Luis Palés Matos ("Topografía")

VOICE CREAKS

oral poem improvised on a smartphone
Cripple Creek, Tallahassee, Florida, 2009

> "Everything
> sleeps here suffocated
> under the dead line that silhouettes
> the rigid and firm level of the fields"

Luis Palés Matos ("Topografía")

El pantano no me espanta
        el bestiario tampoco
se trata del ruido del ambiente
        si bien sin viento
¿en qué condado estamos?
        ¿a qué coordenada
se
        nos
                ha
                        condenado?

The swamp doesn't scare me
        neither does the bestiary
it's all about the surrounding noise
        even though there's no wind
what county are we in?
        we've been sentenced
to
        which
                coordinates?

Between fall and spring
        there is a silence
hardly reciprocal
        the voice I owe to you
is doubtful here
        the voice
is fitful here
        and dodging potholes
because you see
        there are gators here
[it's written like "gat"
        but with an "or" at the end]
I don't count oars
        all I count on
is that voice
        that won't be heard
although
        maybe
            echoing

Entre otoño e invierno
        hay un silencio
poco recíproco
        la voz a ti debida
aquí dubitativa
        aquí voz
como equívoco
        esquivando baches
y es que en el sur
        hay caimanes
[se escribe como imanes
        pero sin la K
o con la K de a-ká]
        tú cuentas 47
yo cuento con la voz
        que no se deja oír
eco
        tal
            vez

. . . como decían del turismo
        pero estoy lejos de la isla
aislado
        si se quiere
este sur
        no es el mío
ni mi norte
        tampoco
cortagramas
        estela de nube
estela de voz
        un muelle
de madera
        a la manera
de tantos otros
        pero irreconocible
en esta
        to
          po
            gra
              fí
            a

. . . they talked about tourism
        but I'm far from the island
isolated
        if you will
this south
        is not my south
nor my north
        really
lawnmowers
        wake of cloud
wake of voice
        a pier
made of wood
        just like so
many others
        yet unrecognizable
in this
        to
          po
            gra
              phy

Hay brisa por fin
       inesperada
voz brisa
       cuerpo brisa
texto brisa
       en la brisa está
la brasa del sentido
       la maquinaria
no deja que se capte
       la presencia
hoy se hace
       penitencia
por estar conectado
       en territorios
con o sin
       incorporar
o
       por
          estarlo

At last there's a breeze
       unexpected
voice breeze
       body breeze
text breeze
       the breeze in
the debris of meaning
       that the machinery
just won't pick up
       the presence
today turning
       to penance
because it's connected
       to territories
that are or aren't
       or long to be
in
       corp
          orated

I don't say hi   instead I greet my gadget   a gadget ritual   that's what I offer
breeze without cool   I recite and I melt   but now that I said that   it's cooling
and it's just that you can't read   the weather here   days as illegible as cries
days of confusion and pragmatism   days of another rhythm   unfinished   hard
to repeat   referring to another instant   another babble   in the fake breeze
another illusion   of expression   is all that I hold
                                                n
                                                t
                                                o

Yo no saludo   o más bien solo al aparato   rito de aparato   eso es lo que
ofrezco   brisa sin fresco   recito y me derrito   ahora que dije eso está enfriando
y es que este clima   no se deja leer   días ilegibles como gritos   días de
confusión y pragmatismo   días de otro ritmo   inconcluso   difícil de repetir
que se remite a otro instante   otro balbuceo   en la falsa brisa   otra ilusión
de expresión   de la que me a
                            g
                              a
                            r
                              r
                              o

Ahora es el zumbido
        de hemisferio
sin estado
        no estatus updates
sin estatuto
        los patos nadan
en el pantano
        ¿será esto quebrada?
¿laguna?
        río no es
no se mueve
        aunque contiene
movi
                miento

Now is the stateless
        hum
of hemisphere
        no status updates
no statute
        the ducks swim
in the marsh
        is this a creek?
lagoon?
        it's not a river
it doesn't move
        although it contains
movemen
                t

. . . that looks like
         a pair of eyes
in the distance
         under the water
I'd say a gator
         but I'd be pushing it
let's say they're eyes
         detached from the voice
that frame a true
         or false relation
with   m
      the   e
         environ
                  t

. . . eso parece
         un par de ojos
a la distancia
         debajo del agua
diría que caimán
         pero sería apresurado
digamos que ojos
         desprendidos de la voz
que marcan una relación
         real o falsa
con
      el
            ambien
                  t
                     e

Me voy moviendo
        en dirección al muelle
hay una silla
        mohosa en el muelle
sin duda los locales
        se escapan
six-pack en mano
        se broncean
se duermen
        los más audaces
saludan al vecino
        ¿qué tal?
                ¿ajá?
                        ¿sí?

Now I'm moving
        toward the pier
there is a rusty chair
        on the pier
no doubt the locals
        escape
six-pack in hand
        and tan themselves
and sleep
        and the more outgoing ones
greet their neighbors
        hey, y'all
                no tallyho
                        . . . see?

Soon the pier
        is going to capsize
but for now
        this tale goes on
and on and on
        toward the territories
of the voice
        mine and the bird's
bird voice
        slurred voice
the voice of false haves
        the one I'm left with
I'm 15 minutes
        away from Georgia
and light-years away
        from nowhere
and yes I know
        I'm sentimental
my only antidote
        against the monu
                mental

Pronto el muelle
        se irá a pique
pero por lo pronto
        la crónica pica
y se extiende
        en los territorios
de la voz
        mía y del ave
ave voz
        voz averiada
la del falso haber
        la que me queda
estoy a 15
        minutos de Georgia
y a años luz
        de ninguna parte
sentimental
        lo sé
único antídoto
        a lo monu
                mental

Este accidente de voz
          este ambiente sin marcas
salvo la que me toca
          cargar y recargar
el aparato define mi canto
          pero no hay batería que valga
para encender la promesa
          de este marrón naranja verde
de este pino avellana
          agua
                    llana

This accident of voice
          these surroundings unmarked
except for the trademarks I carry
          remarks without recharging
this gadget defines my song
          but no battery in the world
can power the promise
          of this brown orange green
of this hazelnut pine
          this water's
                    haze

Island fruits don't grow here
      much less blackberries
but growing are the flows
      of people
of thoughts
      making room for voyages
dislocations
      diasporas
all is displaced
      even in this swamp
that makes invisible
      my gadget's screen
the voice is scared away
      the battery dies
no plug
      no exit
spittle
      falling into the water
returning again
      to the moment of saying
returning to the
      v   o   i   c   e

Aquí no crecen frutos de isla
      mucho menos moras
pero crecerán flujos
      de población
de pensamiento
      donde sea caben destinos
dislocaciones
      diásporas
todo se desplaza
      hasta en este pantano
que hace invisible
      la pantalla de mi aparato
se espanta ya la voz
      se acaba la batería
sin enchufe
      sin salida
saliva
      caída al agua
vuelta de nuevo
      al momento de decirse
de vuelta a la
      v   o   z

DÉCIMAS DEL OTRO MUNDO / OTHERWORLDLY DÉCIMAS

Aguoro tente omi = "revolución en el otro mundo" /
"revolution in the other world" (*Diccionario Lucumí*, Lidia Cabrera)

Ki' = "espíritu de tierra" / "earth spirit"
(*Diccionario Taíno Ilustrado*, Edwin Miner Solá)

[1.0]

No hay que ser espiritista
y haber leído a Kardec
ni conocer a Star Trek
para seguir esta pista;
pregúnteselo al cuatrista
disfrazado de mambí
en taíno y lucumí,
en lucumí y en taíno,
y le mostrará el camino:
aguoro tente omi ki'.

We need not be spirit guides
nor have read Allan Kardec
nor have ever watched Star Trek
to find the ghosts in our stride;
ask **the rebel souls** who cried
singing in **another key**
in Taíno and Lucumí,
in Lucumí and Taíno,
the sorrow songs only **we know**:
aguoro tente omi ki'.

[2.0]

En esta era fantasma
el tecnocapitalismo
ya es parodia de sí mismo
y el planeta tiene asma,
otra nación protoplasma
titubea un ay-de-mí
y apenas se escucha aquí
un silencio cibernético . . .
pero hay un eco profético:
aguoro tente omi ki'.

In this era of predation
and techno**capital**ism
where a laugh track marks each **schism**
toward **the planet's** degradation,
one more protoplasmic nation
will **remix** a woe-is-**me**
to be downloaded for **free**
in the cybernetic stillness . . .
yet **hope echoes through** our illness:
aguoro tente omi ki'.

[3.0]

Canto desde la otra vida
como lo hacía Lavoe
hasta vaciar el yo
como un hermoso suicida
que resucita y anida
en éter de colibrí;
las trizas que descubrí
escombran y dan asilo;
si sabes el resto dilo:
aguoro tente omi ki'.

I sing from **that other** life
like the great Héctor Lavoe
slowly **letting the self go**
like a suicide's jack**knife**
that paints its lovely **red** still life
in the **hum**mingbird's decree;
the stray spirits I set free
shatter us as they **restore** us;
join **me** if you know this chorus:
aguoro tente omi ki'.

[4.0]

En el cuerpo hay un rumor
neural, provisorio y diario
que es el flujo identitario
de revolución en flor,
piel, poro y alrededor,
mundos posibles que vi
bajo el rojo bisturí
del cielo interno y rotundo,
revolución en el mundo:
aguoro tente omi ki'.

Our bodies buzz through the **gloom**
across **neural** viaducts
of identities in flux
and **revolutions** in bloom,
pore and skin and scrawl make room
for **the many worlds** I see
through **the** orbiting **debris**
of a vast internal sky,
revolution's **open eye**:
aguoro tente omi ki'.

[5.0]

Revolución de las alas,
revolución de las noches,
revolución sin derroches,
eufemismos, ni antesalas,
revolución de las balas
en la cuna en que morí,
un abikú y su cemí
en selvas neoliberales
de retoños irreales:
aguoro tente omi ki'.

Revolution of the wings,
revolution of the nights,
revolution that unites
with **the clarity it brings,**
revolution of all things
in **the death cradle** that **claimed me,**
an abikú **and** his cemí
in neoliberal pastures
governed by **unreal masters**:
aguoro tente omi ki'.

MATERIA GRIS / GRAY MATTER

¿Cómo se veía esa ciudad de lejos, desde el avión, al final de la tarde, bajo un sol demasiado alto y entre una maraña de nubes? ¿Cómo se veía su contorno, su ruina colonial bordeando el mar, su chispo de rascacielos, su autopista eterna que da a techitos humildes, urbanizaciones en continua construcción? Materia gris de ciudad.

What would that city look like from afar, from the plane, at the end of the afternoon, under a too-high sky and a tangle of clouds? What would its face look like, its colonial ruin, limning the sea, its itty bit of skyscraper, its eternal expressway that leads to humble rooftops, its subdivisions under constant construction? Gray matter of city.

Eso se preguntaba, mochila al hombro, viendo las pantallas centellear nombres de ciudades como estrellas fugaces en una pecera de mercurio. Todo a su alcance era digital, todo era ajustable, proveía acceso, prometía comunidad, pero la comunidad se había vuelto poco común (o tal vez siempre lo había sido). Ahora se trataba de un vivir incomunicado, con los aparatos como tótemes de un antiguo fetiche, el mismo que anunciaban en las paredes de los edificios hace cien años.

That's what U. wondered, a backpack slung over one shoulder, watching the screens flash names of cities like shooting stars in a pool of mercury. Everything at U.'s disposal was digital, all adjustable, providing access, promising community, but community had become uncommon (or perhaps it had always been so). Now it was all about living in confinement, with one's gadgets as totems of an ancient fetish, the same one advertised on the walls of buildings a hundred years ago.

No es por ser dramático, pero hace tiempo que no veía a nadie. Algunas amistades se habían emparejado en esas maneras socialmente apropiadas tan típicas de cierta clase artística. Otros se habían entregado del todo a su particular fetiche: coleccionar peluches o vestirse de peluche o imaginarse peluche o tener discusiones en foros virtuales sobre la deseabilidad (o no) de los peluches. (Y por peluche entiéndase cualquier valor x; diríamos igual kimono, llavero o alcachofa.) Lo importante era el fetiche. Claro que U. también tenía sus fetiches. Y es que siempre dominaba el deseo: un orden imaginario, un bebé frente al espejo, rumbo hacia el féretro diario. Pero, como veremos, su vida era más forma que contenido (como todas las vidas al fin y al cabo o como la playa con la que soñaba, de acantilados y un cerdo negro salvaje entre las uvas playeras con el monte a la distancia, con la que se calentaba las tripas durante otro invierno en el norte).

Not to be dramatic, but it had been awhile since U. had seen anyone. Some friends had paired off in those socially appropriate ways so typical of a certain artistic class. Others had completely surrendered themselves to their particular fetish: collecting teddy bears or dressing up as teddy bears or imagining themselves as teddy bears or having

debates on online forums about the desirability (or lack thereof) of teddy bears. (And let teddy bear stand for any value x; one might just as well say kimono, key chain, or artichoke.) The important thing was the fetish. Of course, U. also had some fetishes. And it's just that desire always ruled: an imaginary order, a baby in front of the mirror, headed toward the daily coffin. But, as we shall see, U.'s life was more form than content (like all lives, ultimately, or like the beach of U.'s dreams, with cliffs and a black wild pig among the sea grapes with the mountains in the distance, the beach that warmed U.'s belly during another endless northern winter).

Quitándose la mochila y dándole la espalda a las pantallas digitales, pensó que todo era flujo, diáspora, el espacio entre nos y otros, pero en fin un desplazarse, no a la manera histórica de ciertos nómadas peliculeros sino fuera de toda historia memorable, como los zapatos de Andy Warhol graffitiados encima de los de van Gogh (véase Federico Jameson y su lógica cultural del último capitalismo). Pensó en sus propios zapatos: se sujetaban con Velcro en lugar de gabetes, en una especie de guiño juguetón (o desesperado) a sus zapatos de infancia en los años ochenta (¿la nostalgia que describe Jameson?). El Velcro le ahorraba tener que amarrarse los zapatos (y es que la coordinación motora nunca había sido don suyo) pero también le recordaba a un centro comercial de mediados de los ochenta, su padre o su abuela dándole regaños en un carro japonés pequeñito, el mismo sofoque o camiseta batiéndose en la brisa de la tarde, la misma construcción eterna, autopista sin fin, siempre el flujo, siempre el deseo de habitar, de ser habitado.

Now tossing the backpack and turning away from the digital screens, U. started to think that all was flux, diaspora, the space between us and others, but in any case a displacement, not in the historic sense of certain movie nomads, but rather outside of all memorable history, like Andy Warhol's kicks graffitied on top of van Gogh's boots (see Fredric Jameson and his cultural logic of latter-day capitalism). U. thought about U.'s current shoes: they had Velcro straps instead of laces, in a sort of playful (or desperate) nod to the sneakers of U.'s youth in the 1980s (the nostalgia described by Jameson?). The Velcro spared U. the trouble of having to tie shoelaces (it's just that motor skills had never been one of U.'s fortes) but it also reminded U. of a mid-1980s shopping mall, of being scolded by father and grandmother alike in a tiny Japanese car, of that same heatstroke or of a T-shirt fluttering in the afternoon breeze, that same eternal construction, endless expressway, always the flux, always the urge to inhabit, to be inhabited.

Entre hábitat y bitácora escribió en su aparato: *Notas para un texto imposible. Se le iba el avión. Células neuronales. Control muscular. Percepción sensorial. Viendo. Escuchando. Memoria y emoción. Hablando. Despegando.* ¿Cómo se veía esa ciudad sin ojos?

Somewhere between logos and logbook, U. began typing into a gadget: *Notes for an impossible text. U. was going to miss the flight. Neuronal cells. Muscle control. Sensory perception. Seeing. Hearing. Memory and emotion. Speaking. Taking off. How would that city look without eyes?*

HYMNISPHERES   HIMNISFERIOS

Rio de Janeiro / São Paulo, 2009

"and here I respin I begin to project my echo the wreck o recurrent echo of the echoing blow . . ."

Haroldo de Campos, *Galáxias*

(translated by Suzanne Jill Levine,
from a basic version by Jon Tolman)

the raggedness of wonder
keeps us moving
in a rigged system
defined by doubts
and hesitations
somehow in happenstance
of cloud and sandbar
we find our way
through uneasy silences
after the violence
of cities

e aqui me meço e começo e me projeto eco do comêço eco do eco de um começo em eco no de um comêço em eco

la aspereza del asombro
nos mantiene en movimiento
en un sistema arreglado
definido por dudas
y titubeos
de algún modo y de casualidad
de nube y arena
encontramos el camino
entre silencios inquietos
después de la violencia
de ciudades

ahora mirando al mar
sorprendidos por los reflejos
de una mejor moción
está ahí en nuestra canción
ya no una sinceridad fingida
estamos sin estado nuevamente
ingrávidos en la región azul
ya no mirando a casa
pero mirando

e aqui me meço e começo e me projeto eco do comêço eco do eco de um começo em eco no de um comêço em eco

now staring at the sea
blindsided by reflections
of a better kind of motion
it's there in our song
no longer a bluffed sincerity
we are stateless again
weightless in the blue expanse
not looking home
yet looking

now no more than coordinates
numerals and scribbled notions
in ugly bullet points
on a freezing screen
in an Internet cafe
in the middle of a beachfront district
where privilege is bounded by a scarcity
larger than the city
by a scar

e aqui me meço e começo e me projeto eco do comêço eco do eco de um começo em eco no de um comêço em eco

ahora apenas coordenadas
números y nociones garabateados
en viñetas astrosas
en una pantalla congelada
en un cibercafé
en medio de un distrito playero
donde el privilegio se ciñe a una carencia
más grande que la ciudad
una cicatriz

hemos ido lejos buscando empatía
con el cielo y el mar
sólo para hallar la multitud por dentro
el almacén
las resonancias mediáticas
los ensayos para un futuro montaje
doblado y nublado y por fin obnubilado
todavía sin comprender
pero de alguna forma produciendo sentido
de vuelta a los lenguajes
de piel y signo

e aqui me meço e começo e me projeto eco do começo eco do eco de um começo em eco no de um começo em eco

we have come far to commiserate
with sky and sea
only to find the multitude within
the storage room
the sounding board
the rehearsals for a future staging
cast and overcast and finally cast out
still not understanding
but somehow making meaning
returning to the languages
of skin and sign

no longer on the supply side
we are bystanders in the rush of embers
the news cycle stumbles on
drunk on buzz and biz
and clouds reveal the forecast clearing
coming up to the terminus
the trauma

e aqui me meço e começo e me projeto eco do comêço eco do eco de um começo em eco no de um comêço em eco

ya no del lado de la oferta del mercado
somos espectadores en ardor de ascuas
el ciclo noticioso avanza a tropezones
ebrio de rumores y negocios
y las nubes revelan el clarear pronosticado
llegando a la terminal
al trauma

SOLNETO

soneto silábico en escalinata

sol
crisol
o frijol
grito bemol
perdido en el mall
de un downtown sin farol
en la ciudad de aerosol
y arterias de colesterol
postales de otra Sevastopol
interceptadas por la Metropol
en rascacielos de sangre tornasol
Apollinaire degolló soles en alcohol
los contraterroristas soplan su caracol
hologramas digitales de un falso rocanrol

SUNNET

syllabic staircase sonnet

sun
you stun
with your gun
aimed at no one
where car tires spun
now street heat comes undone
like some seventies rerun
burned onto the skin just for fun
and the corpse with its hair in a bun
tells the CEOs who call 9-1-1
"no one is an island but we are all Donne"
while the mall Muzak plays "We've Only Just Begun"
as remixed by the ghosts of La Lupe and Big Pun
and counterterrorists text "son, the enemy has won"

(obituary for the University of Puerto Rico student strike,
2009–10, and for the poet on the sidelines)

HEAVES OF STORM / EMBATES DE TORMENTA

"I heard a Fly buzz—when I died—"
Emily Dickinson

(obituario para la huelga estudiantil de la Universidad de Puerto Rico,
2009–10, y para el poeta en la distancia)

1.

The street is occupied—
    who'll itemize the broken skies?

Sorrow of flags the day you died
    in leased home theaters
only to be reborn in struggle
    like a boldface cry.

Yours is the blue warble of chant
    after the dialectics.

Once the clouds have parted
    you step into the din.

The day you died—
    I heard a Fly buzz.

1.

La calle está ocupada—
    ¿quién enumerará los cielos rotos?

Tristeza de banderas el día que moriste
    en home theaters arrendados
sólo para renacer en la contienda
    como un grito en negrita.

Tuyo es el gorjeo azul del canto
    después la dialéctica.

Una vez clarea el cielo
    te arrimas al estruendo.

El día en que moriste—
    Oí el zumbido de una Mosca.

2.

Entre tenientes
    y terratenientes
existe otra manera
    de tener.

Mantener la mirada
    nombrar el pedregal
examinar la lógica de asedios
    y obedecer lo opuesto.

El viento contraria
    y no obstante aquí hay designio
después de la gesta funesta.

Tu voz retumba
    por todo el hemisferio
filtrando el ocaso convulso
    hasta la cara coraza
de la luna.

La Quietud en el Aire.

2.

Between lieutenants
    and landowners
there is another way
    of owning.

To fix one's stare
    to name the stony ground
to examine the logic of sieges
    and to obey the opposite.

The wind is a contrarian
    and yet there is a plan here
after the ill-fated deed.

Your voice booms
    across the hemisphere
filtering the convulsed twilight
    out to the armor-plate face
of the moon.

The Stillness in the Air.

3.

Suppose we asked
    a different question—
one inspired by your march
    through empire's sunscapes—
Tunis   Cairo   San Juan
    and back to the island sans elixir

The island is a buzzing temporal lobe—
    a wound—the one you carry
in your confusion like an emblem
    a dead language decoded
a shared shudder
    a homeland in absence
a beautiful disquiet—

Between the Heaves of Storm—

3.

Suponte que hiciéramos
    una pregunta distinta—
una inspirada por tu andar
    por los solares del imperio—
Túnez   El Cairo   San Juan
    y de vuelta a la isla sin elixir

La isla es un lóbulo temporal que late—
    una herida—la que cargas
en tu confusión como un emblema
    un lenguaje muerto descifrado
un escalofrío compartido
    una patria en la ausencia
un hermoso desasosiego—

Entre los Embates de Tormenta—

4.

Por un tiempo—nuestro tiempo—
    la tuya fue la verdadera lucha—
sangre y cielo y la canción provisoria
    que volviste tu nuevo lenguaje
una morada morada
    surgiendo de la mara
con miras a dejar ver las entrañas
    del gabán que visten las ratas
bajo el sol multinacional.

Tú y los tuyos se atrevieron a extraviarse
    en la ciudad sin sigilo
hasta verse por fin tras la sombra—
    Y los Alientos se aglomeraban firmes.

4.

For a time—our time—
    yours was the true struggle—
blood and sky and the provisional song
    you claimed as a new language—
a blue-black dwelling
    rising out of the throng
with an eye to revealing the innards
    of the suits worn by the rats
under the multinational sun.

You and yours dared to lose your way
    stealthless in the city
until seeing yourselves as shadows—
    And Breaths were gathering firm.

5.

A thousand years ago
    students claimed the streets
in Paris and Salamanca.

I saw their laughter in yours—
    you who struck and are struck
but were never stricken by fear—
    fear and its strychnine
smiles and screeds
    masking the greed of empire.

And so you stayed—
    like your predecessors
or like flies on a corpse
    reanimating marrow.

The home theater
    is empty now.

Your scream
    pierces the screen
in the hour of coronation—

For that last Onset—when the King
Be witnessed—in the Room—

5.

Hace mil años
    los estudiantes tomaron las calles
en París y Salamanca.

Vi su risa en la de ustedes—
    en huelga de golpe y entre golpes
pero nunca afligidos por el miedo—
    el miedo y sus sonrisas—
diatribas de estricnina
    ocultando la avaricia del imperio.

Y pues permanecieron—
    como sus antecedentes
o como moscas sobre un cadáver
    reanimando la médula.

El home theater
    está vacío ahora.

Tu grito
    perfora la pantalla
a la hora de la coronación—

Para ese último Asalto—cuando el Rey
Se hace presente—en su poder—

6.

Cuando la macana
    descalabra el hemisferio
ojo y lengua se confunden.

Y de esa sinestesia
    nacen los glifos
en las glotis.

Canto-glifos que aseguran
    la verdad sináptica
del sueño compartida.

Tu llave de paso abrió
    el almacén de mi isla.

Yo legué mis Recuerdos.

6.

When the billy club
    splits the hemisphere
eye and tongue blur.

And from that synesthesia
    glyphs are born
in the glottises.

Glyph-songs that vouchsafe
    the synaptically shared
truth of dreams.

Your passkey opened
    the storeroom of my island.

I willed my Keepsakes.

7.

I should have been there with you
    exposed and exposing
or at least making
    noise—jokes—something
instead of mumbling
    this solidarity—

With Blue—uncertain stumbling Buzz
Between the light—and me.

7.

Debí haber estado ahí con ustedes
    expuesto y desenmascarando
o por lo menos haciendo
    ruido—bromas—algo
en vez de balbucear
    esta solidaridad—

Un rumor Azul—incierto tropezando—
Entre la luz—y yo.

8.

Llamémosle no
    universidad
sino *más versos*—
    malversadores somos—
desfondadores.

No sindical
    ni intelectual
sino en el lodazal
    la flor virtual
de tu sonrisa.

Adiós
    carros de piragua—
coco y piña—
    postales del trópico.

Tu tesitura desmiente
    la playa acuartelada.

Caminé hacia tu dulce sismo
    tónico-clónico
sin sistema operativo.

Y entonces las Ventanas fallaron.

    No pude ver para ver.

8.

Let's not call it
    university
but rather *many verses*—
    we are embezzlers—
collapsers.

Neither unionist
    nor intellectual
but rather the virtual flower
    of your smile
in the quagmire.

Good-bye
    snow cone carts—
coconut and pineapple
    postcards of the tropics.

Your stance refutes
    the barracked beach.

I walked toward your sweet
    tonic-clonic tremor
with no operating system.

And then the Windows failed.

    I could not see to see.

9.

Psttt
    hmmm
the buzz
    the zoom
the wah.

The buzz of biz
    the stalled buses
the bass lines
    the battle lines
so many voices in sync.

Return to the dream ache
    the threshing of bones
the urgency
    to be not delivered
but to live without caliber—
    our freedom this tillable land—
an island boundless.

The cut on your lip—
    the sweat drips—
who dreams of this?
    the tirades
the police cars
    technopolis on fire
the high-end mask
    reveals the hollow sneer
of the undercover stiffs.

Yours was the labor of sunlight
    after the chatroom's gloom

not the voice of the voiceless
    instead the mute instrument
of a here and now in harrows—
    the blood current
that anchors archipelagos.

Your hum lifts the sands
    naming the sea
like a hemisphere's echo.

The Stillness—
    and then . . .

9.

Psttt
    hmmm
el zumbido
    el zum
el wah.

El zas del capataz
    los buses detenidos
las líneas de bajo
    las líneas de batalla
tantas voces a la vez.

De vuelta al dolor del sueño
    el trilladero de huesos
la urgencia
    de ser no librado
sino el que vive sin calibre—
    nuestro albedrío este escalio—
isla o confín sin fin.

La cortadura en tu labio—
    el sudor chorrea—
¿quién sueña con esto?
    las invectivas
las patrullas
    tecnópolis en fuego
la máscara más cara
    revela la mueca hueca
de los encubiertos yertos.

Tuya fue la labor del sol
    tras la cibertristeza del chat

no la voz de los sin voz
    sino el instrumento mudo
de un aquí y ahora atormentado—
    la corriente de sangre
que ancla los archipiélagos.

Tu murmullo levanta las arenas
    nombrando el mar
como un eco de hemisferio.

La Quietud—
    y entonces . . .

NOTEBOOK OF A RETURN TO THE NATIVE WALL STREET [INFER-NO-LAND]

Google Translate mashup
of Césaire and Sousândrade

At the end of the morning . . .
(The Republic, having crossed the ANTILLES,

Go away, I told her,
believed to be free of Sheikhs and penetrates

mouth cop mouth cow go away
NEW-YORK-STOCK-EXCHANGE; Voice of deserts :)

I hate minions around bugs and hope.
—Orpheus, Dante, Aeneas, to hell They went down, the Inca's rise . . .

Begone bad gris-gris, bug little monk.
—Ogni sp'ranza lasciate, Entrate Che . . .

Then I turned to paradise for him and his family lost
—Swedenborg, no world to come?

quieter than the face of a woman who lies, and there,
— (Sheikhs laughing and appearing in disguise Railroad-managers, Stockjobbers,
Pimpbrokers, etc. etc..,hawking :)

cradled by the scent of a thought never tired I cherished the wind
—Harlem! Erie! Central! Pennsylvania!

I unlaced watches and could hear the other side of the disaster,
—Million! one hundred million! billion!!

a river of turtledoves and savanna clovers
—Young is Grant! Jackson. Atkinson! Vanderbilts, Goulds Jay, dwarves!

that I always carry in my depths
(The Voice barely heard among the thunder :)

height opposite the twentieth floor houses
-—Fulton's Folly, Codezo's Forgery . . .

the most insolent and as a precaution
—Fraud is the cry of the nation! Odes not understand Railroads; Parallel to Wall-
Street Chattam . . .

against the force putrefying environments
(Brokers continuing :)

twilight surveyed day and night a sacred sun venereum
—Pygmies, Brown Brothers! Bennett! Stewart! Rotschild and ruivalho d'Astor!

At the end of daybreak burgeoning with frail coves Caribbean hungry,
—*Giants, slaves If the nails Well light, is ending up in pain!* . . .

the pockmarked pock Antilles, West Indies blown alcohol, stranded in the
mud of this bay,

(Norris, Attorney; Codezo, inventor, Young, Esq., manager; Atkinson, agent;
Armstrong, agent; Rodhes, agent; P. Offman & Voldo, agents, noise, mirage, the
medium, Guesa :)

in the dust of the city eerily failed

```
            A

      N           M

  A                      E

      C           A

          I
```

ME   REMA

A   EMANA

RICAN   RICA

MAN   CANA

I   NACÍ

CAN   AMÉ

NAME   ME

AN   IRÉ

IRE   AMERICANA

PASTORAL

talking poem—smartphone video
Vacía Talega Beach, PR, 2012

airplanes	por aquí
go by here	pasan aviones
but I'm interested	pero me interesa
in another type of transit	otro tipo de tránsito
another type of trance	otro tipo de trance
happenstance of speaking	percance de hablar
and knowing oneself tired	y saberse cansado
fates afloat	hados al nado
and tongues beside them	y lenguas al lado
syllabaries	silabarios
saliva	saliva
what's left of the sea	lo que queda del mar
briny being	ser salado
stepping aside	hacerse a un lado
wanting to be winged	querer ser alado
transported	transportado
overflowing	desbordarse
in transit	transitar
inciting	incitar
reciting	recitar
undressing	desvestirse
from time to time	de vez en vez
from voice to voice	de voz en voz
without visions	sin visiones
without revisions	ni revisiones
alone	solo
without provisions	sin provisiones
the provisionality	lo provisorio
of this promontory	de este promontorio
of voice	de voz
I'm headed toward	para donde salgo
looking for something	buscando algo
I'm worth as much as	valgo lo que valen
these syllables	estas sílabas
these sounds	estos sonidos
these silences	estos silencios
is there an outlet	¿qué más escape
beyond the vitrine	sino el escaparate
of the machine	de la máquina
where I contemplate myself?	en que me contemplo?
the temple of voice	el templo de voz
I carry within me	que llevo dentro
desecrated	profanado
like this island	como esta isla
without herds	sin ganado
lost territory	territorio perdido
lost thread	perdido el hilo
lost halo	perdido el halo

the hologram	el holograma
amid the mist	entre la bruma
the mist of voice	bruma de voz
of yous	de você
of thous	de vosotros
of others	de otros
of flecks	de trozos
of shreds	de trizas
of traces	de trazos
behind the voice	detrás de la voz
there is another voice	hay otra voz
another symbol	otro símbolo
another piston	otro émbolo
another parenthesis	otro paréntesis
another symptom	otra tisis
another terror	otro terror
another disorder	otro trastorno
burning island	isla horno
heat of voice	calor de voz
shared voice	voz compartida
dispensed voice	voz repartida
departing voice	voz de partida
splayed	de par en par
from skin to skin	de piel en piel
from land to land	de país en país
where no one comes from	de donde no se viene
and no one goes	y adonde no se va
what's left is the machinery	queda la maquinaria
machinations	maquinaciones
all at hand	todo a la mano
instantaneous	todo al instante
but mine is the instant	pero mi instante es
that wanders that staggers	errante tambaleante
stumbling	dando traspiés
without transfers	sin traspasos
mere steps	apenas pasos
mere poses	apenas poses
always here yet	siempre aquí pero
always looking for	siempre en pos de
another city	otra ciudad
without skyscrapers	sin rascacielos
lampposts	postes
nor dance floors	ni pistas de baile
merely an embodied city	apenas ciudad de cuerpo
a city we claim	ciudad propia
inasmuch as alien	en cuanto ajena
a city ours	ciudad nuestra
a city scoured	ciudad muestrario
I'm still here	sigo aquí
between urchin	entre erizos
and eros	y eros
a border being	ser fronterizo
still searching	ser fronte

facing up to	hacerle frente
the difference the refraction	ser diferente refractado
fraction usufruct	fracción usufructo
to be the blanket of breeze	ser la frisa de la brisa
amid all these machines	entre tanta máquina
amid all this disquiet	entre tanto descontento
to be the thirst	ser sediento
to be the sediment	ser sedimento
to be the document	ser pedimento
the mind	ser mente
mind extension of body	mente extensión de cuerpo
machine extension of body	máquina extensión de cuerpo
voice extension of body	voz extensión de cuerpo
machine body	cuerpo máquina
island body	cuerpo isla
continent body	cuerpo continente
hemisphere body	cuerpo hemisferio
collapsing	colapsados
into one another	uno y todos
lapses	lapsos
spacetime	espaciotiempo
without continuity	sin continuidad
discontinuous	discontinuos
in rupture	en la ruptura
in rapture	el rapto
without a locus	sin locus
localized	venidos amenos
in transit	en tránsito
in diaspora	en diáspora
disparate	dispares
dispersed	disparos
disappeared	desaparecidos
the voice I am	la voz que soy
and the voice that I have been	y la voz que he sido

BUZZ   RUMOR

"La erótica lejanía denomina la mecida extensión de lo estelar"

(The erotic distance names the cradled expanse of the stellar)

José Lezama Lima, "Para llegar a Montego Bay"

DESHORACIONES

entre ciudades, 2:22 a.m.

"la kreatibidad de lo ingobernable"

Clemente Soto Vélez (1905–93),
Mujer u ombre u ombre o mujer

1. Mil puertos. **2.** Y algunos más de muertos. **3.** Ahí las coordenadas del sueño. **4.** La mañana del moriviví. **5.** La noche del bosque seco. **6.** La madrugada del eco. **7.** La ecología de soñar. **8.** De despertar. **9.** De un trance a otro trance. **10.** Anclado a la mañana. **11.** Que promete voces y sonrisas. **12.** Pero que no procede. **13.** Vacío el proscenio. **14.** De tu cráneo foráneo. **15.** Te mueves en la cama. **16.** En pesadillas de guerra. **17.** Y tos de invierno. **18.** Hace par de noches. **19.** Te dormías. **20.** Invocando textos sagrados. **21.** Hoy la voz se ha desangrado. **22.** Escribes un poema. **23.** Solo a fuerza de sangrados. **24.** Sinalefas de sin. **25.** Hemistiquios de cero. **26.** Te crees el nuevo poeta de acero. **27.** Sincero en la ciudad futura prometida. **28.** Catalogas desvaríos de hemisferios. **29.** Los blogueros de tu antiguo cautiverio. **30.** Sobreviven inconexos. **31.** En solares sin plexo. **32.** Descapotados y buscando capital. **33.** O sea auspicio. **34.** O sea casa. **35.** Lo del precipicio ya se pasa. **36.** Queda la fiebre. **37.** Tu cuerpo gris bajo colchas tenebrosas. **38.** Prufrock fue célebre. **39.** Pero tú celebras la rebelión de la mano. **40.** Contra las ganas de aplaudir. **41.** Te quitas la barba. **42.** La ropa. **43.** El cero de sincero. **44.** Muestras la cera cincelada. **45.** Tu otro sexo. **46.** Tu animalidad. **47.** Tu dualidad. **48.** La maldición bailable. **49.** La voz voluble. **50.** Tu labia. **51.** Tu aluvión. **52.** Klemente hablaba de la kontradiksión. **53.** Principio de dicción. **54.** Fricción de cuerpos. **55.** No ficciones de facciones. **56.** Sino la extrañeza complementaria. **57.** De donde sale la belleza. **58.** Espontánea. **59.** La hazaña de vivir no es soñar. **60.** Sino hacer del sueño un espacio habitable. **61.** Donde caben los cuerpos. **62.** Vivos y muertos. **63.** Sus injertos. **64.** Te hablé del hemisferio. **65.** Canciones sin voz en estéreo. **66.** Solo un rumor comunicable. **67.** Un rumor compartible. **68.** Enemigo también como el de Lezama. **69.** Pero bordeando el litoral. **70.** Trepando el roquedal. **71.** Un para llegar a. **72.** Una esferaimagen proyectada. **73.** En las galaxias de luz. **74.** Entre el ojo y el planeta. **75.** Soñar entre orbes. **76.** Entre bordes. **77.** Te despiertas en la tarde. **78.** Con recuerdos de un polvo. **79.** Él o ella durmiéndose en tus hombros. **80.** Pero ahora estás solahombre. **81.** Holanombre. **82.** Así saludas a las sombras. **83.** Que a veces te saludan de vuelta. **84.** Entre brisas revoloteando cortinas. **85.** Latas proyectiles rumbo a las calles. **86.** Donde te dejaste querer de noche. **87.** Perdieron tu huella. **88.** Calles de otras ciudades. **89.** Que parecían tuyas. **90.** Ahora te queda apenas ésta. **91.** Ciudad transitoria. **92.** De mugre y alegría migratoria. **93.** Donde sueñas que te enfrentas al pelotón de fusilamiento. **94.** En una silla giratoria. **95.** Te escapas al último momento. **96.** Le cuentas una historia. **97.** De circo y sufrimiento. **98.** De fallo sistémico y falsa gloria. **99.** Vivir escapando. **100.** Ley de la ciudad. **101.** Un vivir escarpado. **102.** Un convivir en el grado cero. **103.** De aceras vacías. **104.** De la ciudad neoliberal. **105.** La que te produjo. **106.** A fuerza del miedo del otro. **107.** Del miedo de sí. **108.** Como

SENTIENCES

between cities, 2:22 a.m.

"de krietíbiti of de ongóbernabol"

Clemente Soto Vélez (1905–93),
Wuman or man or man or wuman

1. A thousand ports. **2.** And many more corpses. **3.** Those are the dream coordinates. **4.** The morning of the touch-me-nots. **5.** The night of the dry forest. **6.** The echo's dawn. **7.** The ecology of dreaming. **8.** Of waking. **9.** From one trance to another. **10.** Anchored to the morning. **11.** That promises you voices and smiles. **12.** Without proceeding. **13.** Bare is the proscenium. **14.** Of your alien cranium. **15.** You're rolling in bed. **16.** In nightmares of war. **17.** And cough of winter. **18.** A couple of nights ago. **19.** You were falling asleep. **20.** Invoking sacred texts. **21.** Today the voice has been bled dry. **22.** You write a poem. **23.** Mostly indented. **24.** Unintended elisions. **25.** Dented sentences. **26.** You think you're the poet unprecedented. **27.** Sincere in your promised city of morrow. **28.** You catalog sorrows of hemispheres. **29.** The bloggers of your ancient captivity. **30.** Surviving unconnected. **31.** In solitary refinement. **32.** Convertible and seeking capital. **33.** In other words sponsorship. **34.** In other words home. **35.** The precipice runs its course. **36.** The fever remains. **37.** Your gray body under dark quilts. **38.** Prufrock was a celebrity. **39.** But you celebrate the hand's rebellion. **40.** Against the desire to clap. **41.** You get rid of your beard. **42.** Your clothes. **43.** Your sincere zero. **44.** You show your chiseled wax. **45.** Your other sex. **46.** Your animality. **47.** Your duality. **48.** Your danceable curse. **49.** Your voluble voice. **50.** Your smooth talk. **51.** Your flood. **52.** Klemente spoke of kontradikshon. **53.** Principle of diction. **54.** Friction of bodies. **55.** Not fictions of factions. **56.** But rather the complementary strangeness. **57.** Where beauty comes from. **58.** Spontaneous. **59.** The feat of living is not dreaming. **60.** But making the dream an inhabitable space. **61.** Where there's room for the bodies. **62.** Living and dead. **63.** As grafted. **64.** I spoke to you about the hemisphere. **65.** Voiceless songs in stereo. **66.** Only a communicable rumor. **67.** A shareable rumor. **68.** Enemy too like Lezama Lima's. **69.** But skirting the coast. **70.** Climbing the rocky shore. **71.** A reaching for. **72.** A sphereimage projected. **73.** In the galaxies of light. **74.** Between the eye and the planet. **75.** To dream amid orbs. **76.** Between borders. **77.** You wake up in the afternoon. **78.** Remembering a lay. **79.** He or she falling asleep on your shoulders. **80.** But girl now you're aloneman. **81.** Helloname. **82.** That's how you greet the shadows. **83.** That sometimes greet you back. **84.** Amid breezes fluttering curtains. **85.** Projectile cans finding the streets. **86.** Where you let yourself be loved last night. **87.** They lost your track. **88.** Streets of other cities. **89.** That seemed to be yours. **90.** Now you're left merely with this. **91.** Transitory city. **92.** Of grime and migratory joy. **93.** Where you dream that you face the firing squad. **94.** In a swivel chair. **95.** You escape at the last moment. **96.** You tell them a story. **97.** Of circuses and suffering. **98.** Of systemic failure and false glory. **99.** Living as escaping. **100.** Law of the city. **101.** Precipitous living. **102.** A coexisting in the degree zero. **103.** Of empty sidewalks. **104.** Of the neoliberal city. **105.** The one

lo ves. **109.** En tu gloria inalámbrica. **110.** Y tu hambre de política. **111.** Tu deseo de ser parte. **112.** Y salvarte. **113.** El arte de zarparte. **114.** Lo aprendiste hace mucho. **115.** En el cuartucho sin luz de tu ciudad. **116.** Oyendo el amor perro. **117.** De los vecinos de arriba. **118.** Él gruñe. **119.** Ella gime. **120.** O al revés. **121.** Las peleas de los vecinos de al lado. **122.** Tirando cosas y gritándose cabrón. **123.** Hasta que una balada de soul. **124.** De los ochenta los silencia. **125.** Por esta noche al menos. **126.** Hasta que queda apenas. **127.** El rumor que te arrulla. **128.** El de los trenes elevados. **129.** Por los rieles bajo cielos. **130.** Crueles de invierno. **131.** Te queda tu silencio. **132.** Casi ininterrumpido. **133.** Por el rumor de un ratoncito en la pared. **134.** O la poesía sonora. **135.** De los televisores. **136.** A las cuatro de la mañana. **137.** Donde la anáfora y el volumen. **138.** Venden horóscopos y cuerpos. **139.** Y mejores erecciones con que poseerlos. **140.** Al menos por un instante. **141.** La ilusión de la noche es que se puede. **142.** Hasta que la mañana trae sus alarmas. **143.** Y café instantáneo con su polvo apresurado. **144.** Y mensajes de texto de camino al trabajo. **145.** Que ya nadie tiene o a punto de perderse. **146.** Pues en esta ciudad todo se pierde. **147.** Todo se pudre. **148.** Todo hecho piedra. **149.** Te despiertas. **150.** Tieso e ileso. **151.** En cuanto iluso. **152.** En cuanto helada la ciudad. **153.** Elisión del signo. **154.** Eleison del cuerpo. **155.** Voz elástica. **156.** Mente hierática. **157.** Neural natural. **158.** Como el hemisferio. **159.** Sur sin norte. **160.** Zurdo sin derecho. **161.** Absurdo atrecho. **162.** De la piel al vocablo. **163.** Y es que cuando hablo. **164.** No soy fiel. **165.** Ni al yo que se desdobla. **166.** Ni al ti que rebota. **167.** Ni al nos que orbita. **168.** Me veo desnudo. **169.** En tu oscuridad. **170.** En la claridad. **171.** Del no verme entero. **172.** En tu afasia. **173.** En la boca. **174.** Que no sacia. **175.** Hemisferio a medias. **176.** Naranja hecha gajo. **177.** Tajo medular. **178.** Autopista y autopsia. **179.** Túmulo de hipotálamo. **180.** Pie forzado de Catulo. **181.** Traspié de polo a polo. **182.** Apología de piel. **183.** Apoplejía de luz. **184.** Cáñamo dañado. **185.** Yo añadido. **186.** Tuyo el superávit. **187.** Nuestro el hábitat. **188.** Dúo excluido. **189.** Tríptico de tripa. **190.** Entre el tú y el yo. **191.** Hay una grieta. **192.** Parecida al sol. **193.** Semejante a la nada. **194.** A la luz caduca. **195.** Atrapada en ciudades. **196.** Menos grises que ésta. **197.** La ciudad sin plata. **198.** Ciudad chata o plana. **199.** Fundada en sueños. **200.** Entre playa y plaza. **201.** Ciudad donde orina uno. **202.** Otro duerme. **203.** Y la especie inerme. **204.** Se desorigina. **205.** Diáspora digital. **206.** De las lúgubres ágoras. **207.** Sin esfera pública. **208.** Ciudad de erratas y escrotos. **209.** De ratas y rotos. **210.** Un dulce terremoto. **211.** Himnos de rabia. **212.** Un convivir remoto. **213.** Un remate. **214.** Un mate. **215.** Un té **216.** Un tú. **217.** Un túnel. **218.** Un hueco. **219.** Un eco. **220.** Uno. **221.** No. **222.** O.

that made you. **106.** Out of fear of the other. **107.** Fear of the self. **108.** As you see it. **109.** In your wireless glory. **110.** And your hunger for a politics. **111.** Your desire to be a part of. **112.** And to save yourself. **113.** The art of setting sail. **114.** You learned it long ago. **115.** In that dark little room of your city. **116.** Listening to the love bites. **117.** Of the upstairs neighbors. **118.** He grunts. **119.** She groans. **120.** Or the other way around. **121.** The fights of the next-door neighbors. **122.** Throwing stuff and calling each other motherfucker. **123.** Until a soul ballad. **124.** From the eighties quiets them. **125.** For tonight at least. **126.** Until all that's left. **127.** Is the rumor that lulls you. **128.** That of the elevated trains. **129.** Over the rails and under. **130.** The cruel skies of winter. **131.** You're left with your silence. **132.** Almost uninterrupted. **133.** By the murmur of a small mouse in the wall. **134.** Or the sound poetry. **135.** Of the televisions. **136.** At four in the morning. **137.** Where anaphora and volume. **138.** Sell horoscopes and bodies. **139.** And better erections with which to possess them. **140.** At least for an instant. **141.** The illusion of the night is that one can. **142.** Until the morning brings with it its alarms. **143.** And instant coffee with its hurried stirrings. **144.** And text messages on the way to the job. **145.** That no one has anymore or is about to lose. **146.** For in this city everything is lost. **147.** Everything rots. **148.** Everything turned to stone. **149.** You wake up. **150.** Stiff and safe. **151.** Inasmuch as dreaming. **152.** Inasmuch as the city is frozen. **153.** Elision of the sign. **154.** Eleison of the body. **155.** Elastic voice. **156.** Hieratic mind. **157.** Neural natural. **158.** Like the hemisphere. **159.** South without north. **160.** Left without right. **161.** Absurd shortcut. **162.** From skin to word. **163.** And it's just that when I speak. **164.** I am not faithful. **165.** To the self that splits. **166.** To the you that ricochets. **167.** Nor to the us that orbits. **168.** I see myself naked. **169.** In your darkness. **170.** In the clarity. **171.** Of not seeing myself whole. **172.** In your aphasia. **173.** In your mouth. **174.** That doesn't satiate. **175.** Hemisphere in halves. **176.** Orange turned to slice. **177.** Cut to the bone. **178.** Highway and autopsy. **179.** Hypothalamus tomb. **180.** Catullus's refrain. **181.** Stumbling from pole to pole. **182.** Apologia of skin. **183.** Apoplexy of light. **184.** Damaged canvas. **185.** Additional self. **186.** Yours the surplus. **187.** Ours the habitat. **188.** Excluded duo. **189.** Gut triptych. **190.** Between the you and the I. **191.** There is a crevice. **192.** Something like the sun. **193.** Similar to nothing. **194.** To the expired light. **195.** Trapped in cities. **196.** Less gray than this one. **197.** The city without cash. **198.** Flat city gashed. **199.** Founded on dreams. **200.** Between beachfront and park bench. **201.** A city where one pisses. **202.** Another sleeps. **203.** And the defenseless species. **204.** Unoriginates itself. **205.** Digital diaspora. **206.** Of the gloomy markets. **207.** Without public sphere. **208.** City of misprints and scrotums. **209.** Of rats and holes. **210.** A sweet earthquake. **211.** Hymns of rage. **212.** A remote coexistence. **213.** An endgame. **214.** A checkmate. **215.** Tea for two. **216.** From me to you. **217.** A tunnel. **218.** A hollow. **219.** An echo. **220.** One. **221.** None. **222.** Done.

UNITED STATES / ESTADOS UNIDOS

American anagrams (via anagram app for smartphone)

STEADIEST NUT	ATTESTED IN US
SEDATEST UNIT	TEST STUN IDEA
SAUTEED TINTS	TEST US DETAIN
TAINTED SUETS	U.S. TAINTED SET
STAIDEST TUNE	TUT SITE SEDAN
TUNE DISTASTE	UNSTATED SITE
SITUATED NEST	SUNDAE TIT SET
UNTASTED SITE	TEASED ITS NUT
ATTEND SUITES	TESTES UNIT AD
TENSEST AUDIT	USE TATTED SIN
ANISETTE DUST	AIDS TEST TUNE
ESTATE NUDIST	TU? SADIST TEEN
ANTSIEST DUET	AUDIT TEN SETS
NASTIEST DUET	SAD SEEN TUTTI
NATTIEST DUES	DUST IT SENATE
SIESTA NUTTED	EDIT AT SUNSET
TASTIEST NUDE	NEATEST STUD I
TAUTNESS DIET	EATEN DUST SITS
TETANUS DEIST	ATTUNED SITES
DENTIST SAUTÉ	STAID TENET US
A STUDENT'S TIE	IS UNATTESTED
A DUSTIEST NET	"ATTITUDENESS!"
SEATED I STUNT	STATES UNTIED

IDEANDO SUSTOS	*ESTADIOS NUDOS*
OSO DESNUDISTA	*NUDISTA SEDOSO*
TISÚS ONDEADOS	*SUDANTE SIDOSO*
DESUSANDO TÍOS	*SUDASTE SONIDO*
SUITES DONADOS	*TENDÍAS SUDOSO*
SUDANDO TIESOS	*TOSÍAS DESNUDO*
SUDANDO ESTÍOS	*SUDAS TOSIENDO*
DEUDAS SIN SOTO	*SUDANTES OÍDOS*
DOSIS ATUENDOS	*SUDANTES ODIOS*
SUDO DESATINOS	*SUDANTE SODIOS*
SUDOSO TIENDAS	*ASENTÍS DUDOSO*
UN O DOS DEÍSTAS	*ODIAS TUS DONES*
¿SU DESTINO? ODAS	*SITUAD SONDEOS*
SUD SO NO DIETAS	*ID USAD SONETOS*
TENIS SO SUDADO	*DESOÍD ASUNTOS*
SITUADOS DONES	*¿DIOSES O TUNDAS?*
TUSANDO DIOSES	*¿NOSIS O DUDASTE?*
SUDAN TEDIOSOS	*EDAD SINO SUSTO*
¿SATINES? DUDOSO	*ENTIDAD SOS USO*
¿TESINAS? DUDOSO	*USANDO DESISTO*
¿SOS ETNIAS? DUDO	*DESUSADO INSTO*
SOSOS TENUIDAD	*ESTUDIO SONDAS*
¿SU SENTIDO? SODA	*DESANIDO SUSTO*

"Queda un mundo plomizo
de fango incierto"

Violeta López Suria (1926–94)

VARIACIONES SOBRE UN PAISAJE
DE VIOLETA LÓPEZ SURIA

VARIATIONS ON A LANDSCAPE
BY VIOLETA LÓPEZ SURIA

"What's left is a leaden world
of uncertain mud"

Violeta López Suria (1926–94)

1.

> lo susurrado es cierto
> > como bruma en la ventana
> > que se abre
> > > de repente
> > > > dejando entrar la ráfaga
> > > no de luz
> > > > sino de ese dulce luto
> > que me devuelve al fango

ALGO DEBÍ DECIRTE   ORFEO   UN ALUMNO DE LA SOLEDAD

1.

what's murmured is true
                    like mist on the window
        that opens up
                        suddenly
                                    letting in a gust
                not of light
                            but of that sweet mourning
        that returns me to the mud

I SHOULD HAVE SAID SOMETHING TO YOU
ORPHEUS   A STUDENT OF SOLITUDE

2.
       incierto, sí
           como lo es el nudo
                  nudo de sí
                         o deseo
               de saberse sonriente
                     en el mundo plomizo
          donde aterrizan pájaros
               en pleno mediodía
            rumbo a los campos
                     donde soltaron
   palabras y gritos
               lenguaje al desnudo
                    desatino de un cuerpo
          de costado al destino
                de camino a la costa

PÁJAROS NEGROS   ME INUNDAN LA MENTE   CON VOCES INSURGENTES

2.

      uncertain, yes
           as is the knot
                  knot of self
                          or desire
             to find oneself smiling
                    in the leaden world
         where birds land
                in the dead of noon
           on their way to the fields
                    where they set free
        words and cries
              language disrobed
                  a blundering body
          sidelong to fate
                en route to the coast

BLACK BIRDS   FLOOD MY MIND   WITH INSURGENT VOICES

3.

        aquí

            los costales de tierra

                      con que cargo, incierto

      de lo que queda del mundo

               soy fango mudo

mudo mi piel a diario

          pronuncio domicilios

                en vigilia y con pesar

     de animal ensamblado

              de ánima digital

circulando el planeta

         planeando

          sobre el cielo prestado

CÓMO COMPARTIR LAS COSAS YA PERDIDAS   CON PERSONAS YA OLVIDADAS

3.

        here go
             the sacks of earth
                       I carry with me, uncertain
of what remains of the world
              I am mute mud
every day I shed my skin
        I pronounce abodes
                  as wakeful and as sorrowful
       as an assembled animal
                   with a digital soul
circling the planet
             gliding
               atop the borrowed sky

HOW TO SHARE THE THINGS ALREADY LOST
WITH PEOPLE ALREADY FORGOTTEN

4.

el roquedal se disuelve
se diluye la raya
que una vez marcó
el ruido de la mañana
entre radio y tormenta

SOLA TORRE   VIAJE DE POCA DURACIÓN
LIBROS AGOTADOS   DÍAS CIRCULARES

4.

the rocky point dissolves
diluted is the line
that once marked
the noise of the morning
between radio and storm

LONE TOWER   SHORT FLIGHT   OUT-OF-PRINT BOOKS
CIRCULAR DAYS

5.

                              sale el sol perseguido
                la tarde ya no ciega
                              se distingue por fin el brillo
        de los edificios
                              como un choque o una fiesta
                una ciudad incierta
                              una sílaba entreabierta
                una voz contraria
                              un desconcierto

FABULACIONES   ALFABETOS   DESDOBLAMIENTO   SUEÑO   MUNDO

5.

                                     the persecuted sun rises
            the afternoon no longer blinds
                                at last one can make out
        the sheen of buildings
                                like a crash or a party
            an uncertain city
                                    a syllable ajar
                    a contrary voice
                                    a disconcerting

6.

desplomarse plomizo
  dormir por semanas
 despertar en la grama
   de un estadio abandonado
y decirse sin pensarlo:
   "queda un mundo plomizo"
y darse cuenta de que el mar
    está hecho de granizo
el tiempo es un gran hechizo
   y el espacio otro conjuro

6.

a leaden collapse
        to sleep for weeks
    to wake up on the grass
      of an abandoned stadium
and to say without thinking:
     "what's left is a leaden world"
and to realize that the sea
          is made of hail
time is a mighty spell
    and space another incantation

REPERTOIRE OF SONG   AFTER THE SOCIAL FALLACY

7.

no hay códigos

                    sino colores

que se borran en el cráneo

            lo percibido es un ruido

                        excedente del ambiente

        sucesiones de heliotropos

                un derroche de muebles

        un silencio de pianos

                            espaciotiempo

    simultáneodiscontinuo

                        oriundoforáneo

                    un proscenio

                    un peldaño

7.

                    there are no codes
                                    only colors
            that wash out in the cranium
                    what's perceived is a noise
                                        the environment's remains
                succession of heliotropes
                                    a profusion of furniture
                    a silence of pianos
                                            spacetime
            simultaneousdiscontinuous
                                        nativeforeign
                            a proscenium
                                            a step

8.

no todas las violetas son flores
no todas las flores violeta
pero pronto es primavera de nuevo en la ciudad
pronto nos besamos
nos vemos centellear
en el fango cotidiano
en ti soy un mundo
no el que pasa incierto,   plomizo
¿será que el guitarrón
se hizo desierto
se deshizo en la marea
y naufragó en manos
más pequeñas que las nuestras
para mostrarnos el camino
sin academia
sin instituto
a orillas del parque
de la palabra hecha voz?

8.

        not all violets are flowers
                 not all flowers are violet
but soon it is spring once again in the city
    soon we kiss
             we see ourselves sparkle
      in the everyday mud
      in you I am a world
not the one that goes by uncertain,   leaden
    could it be that the mammoth guitar
              became a desert
      dissolving in the tide
         and wrecking in hands
     smaller than ours
          showing us the way
      without academy
          without institute
    toward the edge of the park
        where word becomes voice?

WORD MADE OF EARTH   OF MUSIC   CONTINENT OF MEMORY

9.

un mundo plomizo de fango incierto
(lo que queda del ámbito seguro),
ya pronto la academia del futuro
nos abrirá sus puertas como un puerto

y entraremos cual larva en el injerto
de la sociedad ya hecha cianuro:
tú ahí junto al umbral, cabeciduro,
yo con mi delantal de mar abierto . . .

seremos ceremonia del ahogado
por esos venenosos litorales
de otra ínsula así, como la nuestra:

detritus de gomera, matorrales,
dos féretros del mar descapotado
orbitando por la ciudad ancestra.

ME CONFORMÉ AL OIRTE
CORO ELECTRÓNICO   DE RAÍCES OSCURAS   COMPARTIDAS

9.

a leaden world, uncertain mud, in short,
what little is left of the bulwarked sphere,
the academy of the future nears
and opens us its doors just like a port—

we'll glide right past the cyanide resorts
like larvae nesting in the social sneer:
you, under the threshold, stubborn and clear,
me in my open sea-apron of sorts . . .

we'll be the ceremony of the drowned
across venomous coastlines wide and far
in some such other island just like ours:

car-tire detritus and scrubland scar,
in top-down seas we're two coffins unbound
orbiting the ancient city's towers.

I WAS CONTENT ONCE I HEARD YOU
ELECTRONIC CHORUS   OF DARK ROOTS   SHARED

MAJOR TOM (COMING HOME)

Syracuse, NY

the answer song to space oddity plays in downtown
cafes in all the cities of the planet undiscovered still the
harmonizing *whoas* over the drum shuffle the side streets
with tags illegible *rest in peace* in blood red next to the
dilapidated wood frame you see there is no peace in the
post-postindustrial north except in pieces here where
ricans once settled now students scuttle and the tech
sector thrives bio-less preserved in the gray bile of spring
with no bayous no *caballos* only some cobblestones amid
the cable modems now that the *x-vox* hides a body in the
north but far from this cafe we come here and survive
against all odds like the phil collins song that plays
now only who would take a look at you now while you
take a leak in a cafe that oozes hand sanitizer or against
a mirrored wall overhearing interns without glamour
discuss digital code and their muffled love lives like in
that phil collins song going on too long now wondering
who'll take a liking to me now that there's just an empty
space now that decaf and decay begin to sound the same
when spoken into a smartphone now that the RED BULL
is gone and in its place is a DRUBBED BELL a DULL URB a
LUBED DUDE a RUBBER BUD a DUBBED RULER a URL RUBE a
REED a BULB a LULL a BURB a DUEL a RUDE BLURB a BLUE
BURBLE a BLUR a BUBBLE in the RUBBLE

FAKE FLOWERS   [after Alurista: a Rican rikka]

Wassup,
    raza
qué pasa,
    my peeps?
insipid
líquido de
brain valve
aneurisma
  vuelve
anota
oprime
  prime numbers
on the face
of stucco buildings
  elevator chute
shaft
      damn!
gente
con vista
    20/20
behind
venetian blinds
improperly
partitioned
the programmatic
  handclaps
of the safely
  prerecorded
heretofore
unheard
  aplauso manco
banco de
    datos
what's that?
it's fact
into free flow
    [dat's capital]
it always
rains in cali
this time
of year

I heard the
mayor say
"this year
things
are gonna
go our way
we're due"
    dime tú, dude
    si no es
  cierto
where to now?
fake blues
in downtown clubs
you've never
    heard of
    here
have you?
aquí no se habla
      así
    se dice aquello
que queda
de mañana
    5 AM
street sign
rough trade
  de callejón
post-industrial
    latté factories
are shutting down
this year again
to disappear
the moon
at last
to have it fold
    into the sea
  como quien
convoca gente
the pitter-patter
of tiny fiats
in queens gate
or plaza square

the circle line
mayorista
al por menor
  detal
    astilla
don't wanna be ya!!
vaya qué villas
  y castillas!
    noches de pastillas
en el sur de francia
that côte d'azur
you wear it well
like turtlenecks
displayed each
open mic nite
by the gutter punk m.c.
with ph.d.s
    up to his rabo
  al cabo de
    unos días
this free disease
will cost you
  something
death by degrees
art décor architexts
in morgue light
that's entertainment
    the people you meet
SPLITTERS!
  SPLINTERS!
hip banter
    beep beep:
"leave mess intact"
omission viejo
  turn off
next exit
  burn off
  the calories
la grasa
  saturada
  in the park

se dice
logros
  se dice
gracias
    se dice *grammar*
      of remembering
crib-sheeted again
  se dice *does*
    se dice *was too!!*
      nah-uh!!!
air jordans
  how 90s!
members only jackets
  how 80s!
pet rocks
. . . you get the picture
LANGSAM!
you get for me algo
  se dice grassy ass
    se dice *sin tax*
for my peeps,
          reprazent!!!
represas!
          damn u
fine!
reappraise meaning
& maybe you'll
        come up w. something
similar to
"reappraise"
        el rey de harlem
means no harm
he's crowned in
  corona
  boston-born
in heady pilgrimage
and moving en route
  to secaucus
to be buried
  to montpelier
to be married
you see I too can write
vermont notebooks

dare me!
      pa que veas
the packet boats
        are docking
the sunset
      is real
this time around
      ask around
        and you'll see
it's all about
      self-as-other
      ser en sí
y en pos de
        depositions
de post-its
        posters on the
depot's postes
      pos-ter-GA-do
that's my street form   [42 day]
      uniforme cuneiforme
war-torn cathedral
citizens asunder
presidential underwear
      "el drama de las masas
      hermosas y asesinas"
everyone's gone to the movies
      popcorn armrest
floor gunk   uncomfortable
      bathroom encounter
matinee with 8-track music
filling station   pastorality
              americana soundz
un poco así   like flight
        you know the rest areas
        "we the peepholes!"
emblems of phlegm
to bethlehem   [pa. & back]
this unsaid movement
        diasporous
                nosostracized
nos: not *sever*
      lo mismo quial
                    revés

YOU HAVE THE NICE WEATHER

after a sonnet by Sor Juana Inés de la Cruz

In Tennessee you phone book. You use me? Sucks.
In get still friends. One before leaving bro.
For me an ass off. Send me and send the info.
You know me and in the me. Las Vegas us.

Doing with the mall the sodas. Progress sucks.
Yeah C.C. on outside. Moscone Center.
When you get up, do you do me and?
So you know an inconvenience ass kicker sucks.

Email to the animal so Karen see there.
This this will see you. Benefit added.
Do you think it's a matter of cream and be there?

Any and go for me tomorrow. Read about this.
Cancel me? Too funny! I'm gonna be there.
Get on some you. I love you there. In bunny rabbits.

¿En perseguirme, mundo, qué interesas?
¿En qué te ofendo, cuando sólo intento
poner bellezas en mi entendimiento
y no mi entendimiento en las bellezas?

Yo no estimo te**SOR**os ni riquezas,
y así, siempre me causa más contento
poner riquezas en mi entendimiento
que no mi entendimiento en las riquezas.

Y no estimo hermosura que vencida
es despo**J**o civil de las edades
ni riq**U**ez**A** me agrada feme**N**tid**A**,

teniendo por mejor en mis verdades
consumir vanidades de la vida
que consumir la vida en vanidades.

SCENE APPS

The Greeks had represented the soul outside of the body in the form of a small ghost, keeping the likeness of the body, or in the guise of a small nude figure, winged and always painted black. It seems that the latter mode of representation of a spiritual substance guided Christian artists in their early representations of the devil, which is reproduced in the form of a kind of genie, of a small nude being, sometimes winged, coming out from either the mouth or the skull of the exorcised.

QUIT   WORTHWHILE   PREMIER   PATROLMAN   TIRED   SYMPATHY
PERISH   BIGOT   MORE   PREAMBLE   ADVENT   SMALL-TIME
VERY   SHOVE   SEXUALLY   STYROFOAM   FIGURE OF SPEECH   IMITATE
SLAIN   SKINTIGHT   OVERT   GROCERIES   TINGLING   MARATHON
HELPFULNESS   GUN   JET-PROPELLED   TURNIP   SUNLIT   CHASTITY
GOODNESS   ELEGY   NEAT   FRISBEE   PORNOGRAPHER   SEEM   ENERGY
INTERCHANGEABLE   FORM   LETTER   WHITEN   DONATION   SUPERIOR
CHORD   ASTUTELY   LITIGATE   ARBITER   ANTONYM   ONE-NIGHT STAND
CHECKPOINT

Later on, that figure of the exorcised takes on more accurate strokes, the demon has horns, a tail, claws, and he even takes the forms of the strangest of animals; and, even among the great artists of the Renaissance, we find a nod to this tradition, in the form of some small devils in a corner of the painting. But here the symbol becomes incidental and the demoniac himself possesses those grippingly realistic hallmarks that we will emphasize throughout the book, in the context of sixteenth-century painting.

DEJAR   PATRULLERO   PREMIER   PENA   SIMPATÍA   CANSADO   PERECEN   MÁS
INTOLERANTE   ADVENIMIENTO   PREÁMBULO   DE POCA MONTA   MUY   EMPUJÓN
SEXUALMENTE   CIFRA   DE ESPUMA   DE POLIESTIRENO   DE EXPRESIÓN   IMITAR
ASESINADO   AJUSTADOS   COMESTIBLES   ABIERTAS   HORMIGUEO   UTILIDAD
MARATÓN   PISTOLA   DE CHORRO   DE PROPULSIÓN   NABO   CASTIDAD
ILUMINADO POR EL SOL   BONDAD   PORNÓGRAFO   ELEGÍA   ORDENADO
FRISBEE   PARECER   LETRA   ENERGÍA   FORMA   INTERCAMBIABLE
BLANQUEAR   ACORDE   DONATIVO   SUPERIOR   ASTUTO   LITIGAR   ANTÓNIMO
ÁRBITRO   DE UNA MESITA DE NOCHE   PUESTO DE CONTROL

The convulsion of the eyeballs, wherein the pupils tend to hide under the upper eyelid, is a very characteristic trait of the attack of convulsive hysteria and one that we will see attributed to the best artists. Tense eyebrows and forehead wrinkles express suffering; the nostrils are visible and the mouth, wide open, reveals the teeth. It is this in particular that attracts the attention of the characters positioned to the right: their faces express astonishment, horror, and disgust.

UNDERGO   BAT   FONT   FOLK   CREEK   GULCH   JIG   PRURIENT
PITTANCE   DIVERGENCE   ROCK   ROUNDABOUT   SELF-IMPROVEMENT
HUNKER   DEODORANT   CADET   DIAGNOSIS   PEACEABLE   FREEZING
POINT   WHORE   PRODIGAL   REPUGNANT   GRAFT   GRANNY   UNPLEASANT
AFFECT   EXHALE   QUARTERS   VIOLENTLY   CAMPING   REPATRIATION
WAITING ROOM   SYNTHETICALLY   STUPOR   CIVIL LIBERTIES   MATCHLESS
AFAR   PERPETRATE   FLAKE   OVERSIMPLIFY   MYSTICAL   DOG-EARED
TESTIFY   SUPERBLY   ORIGINATE   SCARED   SHOULD   CURSED   COLORBLIND

We find there, indeed, several characteristics of the beginning of a major hysteric attack. It seems that the moment chosen by the painter is that when the attack begins and before the major convulsions. In scientific terms, we could say that the patient is in the first stage or epileptoid stage of the attack. It would be possible to specify more and even to add that she is in the phase of tonic spasm.

SOMETEN   FUENTE   BATE   POPULAR   ARROYO   BARRANCO   PLANTILLA
LASCIVO   MISERIA   DIVERGENCIA   ROCA   ROTONDA   DE SUPERACIÓN
HUNKER   DESODORANTE   CADETE   DIAGNÓSTICO   PACÍFICO   PROSTITUTA
PUNTO DE CONGELACIÓN   PRÓDIGOS   REPUGNANTES   INJERTO   ABUELITA
DESAGRADABLES   AFECTAN   CUARTOS   EXHALA   VIOLENTAMENTE   ACAMPAR
SALA DE ESPERA   REPATRIACIÓN   SINTÉTICAMENTE   LAS LIBERTADES CIVILES
ESTUPOR   ESCAMA   INCOMPARABLE   PERPETRAN   LEJOS   SIMPLIFICAR
DEMASIADO   MÍSTICO   MANOSEADO   TESTIFICAR   MAGNÍFICAMENTE   ORIGINAN
MIEDO   DEBE   MALDIJO   DALTÓNICO

Seized by her malady, the young woman falls backwards, and stiffness has already invaded her entire body. This fall has nothing to do with the muscle weakness of syncope or fainting. We feel that this body curved backwards is stiff from head to toe. The slightly bent legs are spasms, as evidenced by the convulsed feet with the toes sticking out. The head, bent forcefully backwards, brings out the swollen neck, and the face, all puffy and turgid, betrays the interrupted breathing brought about by the generalized spasm. The two arms diverge from the trunk as if to undertake these great tonic movements that we will describe later on. It is true that, according to our hypothesis, the fingers should be bent in palm of the hand and the forearm in pronation instead of supination. But the right hand in the fresco is obviously tense, more than our drawing can show.

SAGEBRUSH   LUMBERJACK   INSIPID   CROSSFIRE   STREET   RECORD   HORRIBLE
DRAGON   TERRACE   INFLAME   OKAY   VOYAGE   ALLOTMENT   DELIRIUM
MUSEUM   TRANSCRIBE   GARGANTUAN   WON   MELT   INDISCRIMINATE
HIGH SCHOOL   LUKEWARM   RECKLESS   TAXABLE   CARBON PAPER   TYPICAL
EXPECTATION   PUS   CHOPPY   EXTRAVAGANCE   TO AND FRO   ABORTION
URBAN RENEWAL   TRASH   APPLICABLE   FOLK   MYSTICAL   TUMULT
FRICTION   MIDNIGHT   STEPDAUGHTER   CONSUMPTION   OAF   AFTERSHAVE
REVERSAL   UNBUTTON   REGULATION   SOLD   REEDUCATION   PRINCIPALITY

All these characteristics do not represent true epileptic fits, but they belong undoubtedly to this phase of the great hysterical attack which sometimes resembles the very similar epileptic fit and which we are calling the epileptoid stage. Above the image of the possessed woman, two small winged devils flutter.

*LEÑADOR ARTEMISA INSÍPIDO FUEGO CRUZADO CALLE TERRAZA RÉCORD
TERRIBLE DRAGÓN INFLAMAR ADJUDICACIÓN VIAJE VALE TRANSCRIBIR
GIGANTESCO MUSEO DELIRIO GANÓ FUSIÓN INDISCRIMINADA ESCUELA
SECUNDARIA TIBIA IMPRUDENTE IMPONIBLE EXPECTATIVA PAPEL CARBÓN
TÍPICO PUS EXTRAVAGANCIA PICADO UN LADO A OTRO ABORTO BASURA
RENOVACIÓN URBANA APLICABLE MÍSTICA POPULAR TUMULTO FRICCIÓN
MEDIANOCHE HIJASTRA CONSUMO ZOQUETE INVERSIÓN PARA DESPUÉS DEL
AFEITADO UNBUTTON REGULACIÓN VENDIDO PRINCIPADO REEDUCACIÓN*

In the upper part of the body, the signs of seizures are fanciful and contradictory. Despite the distortion of the eyeballs, the physiognomy is not that of a subject in a critical state. The wide-open mouth seems to blurt out loud cries, which would be contrary to the state of generalized spasm, wherein the stiffness that invades the upper extremities tends to take hold. Moreover, this convulsion is itself not natural. The right arm is raised vertically, the hand in a pose that is academic yet lacking in character. The left arm is lowered, all the muscles are drawn into violent projections, the wrist is extended, the fingers are spread and forcibly extended. There are myriad ways of representing how a member is affected by a process of convulsive attacks, as we can see in other works; the way in which it was represented by Raphael is perhaps the only one we have not had the opportunity to observe. We know that the most frequent posture of the hand is in forced flexion of the wrist and fingers with an exaggerated pronation, while the forearm is extended.

*TARMAC COWBOY VETERAN INFAMOUS WALK-UP EGALITARIAN
ANTHROPOLOGIST WILLOWY DAINTILY BEAT WATER BED FIGURE OF SPEECH
COAT TRANSSEXUAL GUNPOWDER CLEAN-SHAVEN SADLY DIPLOMATIC
EYE SHADOW ARISTOCRATIC LACKING ACQUAINTED EFFECTS OVERHAND
STRAGGLE FORTIFICATION LIFELINE AGGRESSIVENESS INTERPLAY
AGREEABLY GENERAL ELECTION TURBULENT METABOLIC SHIMMER
INTERWOVE METROPOLITAN LYRICS INSTEP COURTEOUS KEEPER
SPURN GRANDMA CANNED NEST ADAPT CURSOR ACKNOWLEDGED
ARRAIGNMENT NITTY-GRITTY CREATIVE*

The head is tilted to the left, revealing an agitated physiognomy: the eyeballs are convulsed downward and at the same time squinting inward, and the mouth is half-open in an observably convulsive movement. In sum, we find in this figure, obviously taken from nature, several signs that belong undoubtedly to the convulsions of hystero-epilepsy.

*ASFALTO VETERANO VAQUERO INFAME WALK-UP ANTROPÓLOGO ESBELTA
FIGURA IGUALITARIA DELICADAMENTE GOLPEAR CAMA DE AGUA DE LA
CAPA DISCURSO PÓLVORA TRANSEXUAL BIEN AFEITADO SOMBRA DE
OJOS CON TRISTEZA DIPLOMÁTICO ARISTOCRÁTICA CARECE DE EFECTOS
FAMILIARIZADOS OVERHAND SALVAVIDAS STRAGGLE FORTIFICACIÓN
INTERACCIÓN AGRESIVIDAD ELECCIONES GENERALES AGRADABLEMENTE
TURBULENTO METABÓLICO BRILLO ENTRETEJIÓ METROPOLITANA PORTERO
EMPEINE LETRAS CORTÉS RECHAZAR NIDO ABUELA CONSERVA
ADAPTARSE CURSOR RECONOCIDO ARRAIGO MEOLLO DE LA CUESTIÓN
CREATIVA*

In the foreground, Rubens placed, in a bold shorthand, a man possessed, almost naked, lying on the ground, and who, in a terrible convulsion, broke the ties that had bound him. This figure, which is not present in the Genoa painting, is no less remarkable than the one we have studied in detail. The turned head reveals a dreadfully convulsed face. The eyes are distorted, the pupils convulsed upward, the mouth is open, the lips are blue and foamy.

COUNTERFEIT PACIFISM RESONANCE THEM ILLUSTRATE RICH ONE-TRACK MIND SELF-STARTER DEVOTION NUCLEUS ZIP CODE WALL-TO-WALL SCHMOOZE PARENTAL LUNAR OFFER CONTRABAND SIZZLE MASS WESTERNER MINUSCULE BENCHMARK RETREAT WARSHIP JILT CARELESSLY GRAY MATTER CHALK WRONGFUL TWIN-SIZE GIG CUSTOM-BUILT SHIN UNBROKEN STOPOVER GENTLEMAN RETRIBUTION LEWD EGO SNEAK UNKEMPT PAPER EDIFICATION RINSE FOREARM DATA AUDIOVISUAL PROVISIONAL LOVESICK

In its attitude and its movements, this figure feels affected, an imitation of the master. But it would be unfair to ignore the features by which the artist has sought to reproduce nature. The posture of both hands, among others, seems inspired by the demoniac art of Rubens, of the Vienna Museum.

RESONANCIA PACIFISMO FALSO ILUSTRARLOS RICO DE UNA SOLA PISTA MENTE ARRANQUE AUTOMÁTICO NÚCLEO DEVOCIÓN CÓDIGO POSTAL DE PARED A PARED SCHMOOZE PADRES CONTRABANDO OFERTA LUNAR CHISPORROTEO OCCIDENTAL MASA DE REFERENCIA MINÚSCULO BUQUE DE GUERRA RETIRO JILT TIZA DESCUIDADAMENTE MATERIA GRIS ILÍCITO DE DOBLE TAMAÑO PERSONALIZADO CONCIERTO CONSTRUIDO CABALLERO ESPINILLA ESCALA ININTERRUMPIDA RETRIBUCIÓN SNEAK LASCIVO EGO DESCUIDADO EDIFICACIÓN PAPEL ENJUAGUE DATOS DEL ANTEBRAZO ENFERMO DE AMOR PROVISIONAL AUDIOVISUAL

LANGÚ

ageless language;
after LaTasha N. Nevada Diggs

I'm always **siempre tengo pesadillas**
having nightmares **moozhag ingiiwashkwengwash**

Niin inwewin I'm language **soy lenguaje**
babaa-ayaa dando vueltas wandering

My brain **niinindib cerebro**
it makes **madwewe ruido** noise
apii cuando choca con when it hits **bitaakosin**
aki la tierra the earth
hello! **boozhoo! hola!**

Mi tierra aki my land is what **lo que me viene**
comes to mind **a la mente mikwendaagwad**
niiyaw de mi cuerpo of my body
al gaguear as it stutters **gagiibanagaskwe**

Ombiigizi tierra my noisy earth **mi ruidosa aki**
is recollected **mikwendan es un andar**
babaa-ayaa rememorado wandering

Soy nilnltam inwewin ruidoso I'm noisy language **lenguaje ombiigizi**
land of body **tierra del cuerpo niiyaw aki**
gagiibanagaskwe gagueando un stuttering **boozhoo! hola!** hello!

noise memory language land brain body
agimediruni abadi iñeñei mua sesu úgubu
noise memory language land brain body
babel memoria idioma pais selebre kurpa
noise memory language land brain body
napituruk itqaqtuq uqautchit nuna qaqisaq timi
noise memory language land brain body

✿ ✿ ✿ ✿ ✿ ✿ ✿ ✿ ✿ ✿

AYMBERÊ
BAQUARA
CANHEMA
DANONO
ESSÁ
GOITACÁ
IRA
JUCASSABA
KAMBY
MORAUSSUBA
NHENHENHÉM
ORÉ
PAUÁ
QUICÉ
RECÔ
SOO
TOBÁ
UIRÁ
VAPIDIANA
WARIWA
XE
YBAPIRANGA

A wise lizard
fleeing the
ceremony.

A nomad eye:
honey of
death

    or milk of love.

We say it
all: home
is

    a dull knife

against our animal faces.

We are a
tribe of
apes:

    mine

is the red sky.

* * * * * * * * * *

ANDAYA
CHIYO
DACAA NAA NUHU CA ÑUU
EL SOL
FEBRERO
HUAHI YEQUE
INI
JISIYUU
LLODZO CASTILLA
MINI
ÑUHU
PICIETL
QUIVUI
RENDACA
SATA
TAA
UVUI
VIDE ABRIR
XITON
YAA ÑUHU

The underworld's foundation
from all
eternity.

The February sun:
sepulcher heart,
field,

    hollow pen, tobacco fire.

To be born
a bee
in

    the beyond.

To write. Two.
To open
the

    merchant god's

tongue of fire.

✿ ✿ ✿ ✿ ✿ ✿ ✿ ✿ ✿ ✿

ANVIRON
BYENNERE
CHANTE
DEVANJOU
ENSTIGE
FLANM
GÒJE
HANCH
IL
JI
KONESANS
LANG
MEZI
NASYON
ÒFELEN
PÈP
RAMAN
SANBLE
TANPÈT
UNI
VWAYAJ
WÈ
YÈ
ZÈWO

Around **b**lissful **c**hants
dawn **e**ntices
flame

    gulping **h**ip **i**sland **j**uice.

Knowing **l**anguage's **m**easure:
nation's **o**rphan
people

    rarely **s**imilar.

Tempests **u**nite **v**oyagers
witnessing **y**esterday's
zero.

RUMOREDS   HER HEMISPHERE IN ME

for my mother and her struggle

el abdomen azul de la madre   **the mother's blue abdomen**   la máquina
entre flores   **the machine wreathed in flowers**   la cablería del cielo   **the
hardwired sky**   la corriente alterna   **the alternate current**   del otoño y
sus estacionamientos   **of autumn and its parking lots**   el juicio lento del
árbol sin pájaros   **the slow trial of the birdless tree**

el gotereo de los sures   **the leaky souths**   el fusil de los nortes   **the
trigger-happy norths**   y a lo lejos la comida de hospital   **and hospital food
in the distance**   alitas fritas con sabor a microondas   **microwaved fried
wings**   la amable fetidez de las sonrisas   **the nice and fetid smiles**   el
aroma a pasillo en un planeta de pasillos   **the smell of hallways in a planet
full of hallways**   donde recibes la alerta desde el otro lado   **where you get
the warning from the other side**   la señal de las viudas insomnes   **the
signal from the sleepless widows**

tu experimento en mentalismo   **your mind's-eye experiment**   comienza con
la conciencia descapotable   **begins with the convertible conscience**   la
música que te habita   **the music that inhabits you**   que nombra tu masa
púrpura   **that names your purple mass**   los vasos conductores todos
tiemblan sobre el alero   **the communicative vessels tremble on the ledge**
se inflama la forma sin memoria   **the form without memory is now swollen**
como una calle llena de ratas sorprendidas   **like a street full of rats**   por
la luz de los helicópteros   **stunned by the light from the helicopters**   que
vienen de islas cercanas   **that come from nearby islands**   a tomarle fotos
al silencio de tu primera noche   **to take pictures of your first night's silence**
a documentar la pérdida   **to document loss**   como historiadores del miedo o
poetas forenses   **like historians of fear or forensic poets**

queda tu ceño amarillo   **what remains is your yellow brow**   la bata
larga y sucia de lo que no se nombra   **the long and dirty nightgown of the
nameless**   la foto que no se toma   **the photo no one took**   porque se sabe

todo lo que no se sabe   **because everyone knows what no one knows**   me
preguntas por qué no te grabé   **you ask me why I didn't record you**   esa
primera noche de despedidas   **that first night of goodbyes**   de amistad con
el velo   **of making friends with the dark**   cuando llegaste a la pulsión plena
when you reached the stark drive   fuiste animal vegetal mineral   **you
were animal vegetable mineral**   y al fin maquinal   **and finally machinic**
función de sodio y oxígeno   **a function of sodium and oxygen**

me despedí con los Beatles   **I said goodbye with the Beatles**   pensé en
como siempre te lamentabas   **I thought about how you always regretted
being**   de ser la única en tu familia que cantaba feo **the only one in your
family who couldn't sing**   y en como siempre encontré tu voz linda   **and
how I always found your voice pretty**   por el esfuerzo   **in its exertion**
por como te empujabas para llegarle a la nota   **in how you would strain to
reach a note**   como esa noche te empujaste   **just as you pushed yourself
that night**   de un techito a otro techito   **from one rooftop to another**
como quien quiere ver el mar una última vez   **like someone longing to see
the sea one last time**   como quien quiere despedirse sin pedir permiso   **like
someone intent on leaving without asking for permission**   pero no sin
antes flotar   **but not without first floating**   en lo amniótico que le precede
al sol   **in the amniotic substance that precedes the sun**   esa otra estrella
que estalla   **that other star that bursts**   sobre la pared agujereada   **on
the riddled wall**   por donde pasan los cuerpos como formas   **where bodies
cross like forms**   de aire sin deletrear   **made of unspelled air**   como
rumor   **like a murmur**

y es que de ti heredé el hemisferio   **and it's just that I inherited your
hemisphere**   la mano zurda que se cree diestra   **the left hand that
believes itself right**   la ansiedad no de estar vivo sino de estar   **the anxiety
not of living but of being**   hijo de tu malestar   **a child of your malaise**
diáspora prematura   **premature diaspora**   la convulsión febril de mi dualidad

the febrile seizure of my duality   bilingüe bisexual ambidiestro   **bilingual bisexual ambidextrous**   vivo en la dualidad del signo   **I live in the duality of the sign**   en la isla que somos y no somos   **in the island that we are and that we aren't**   en la ciudad que nos acoge y nos mata   **in the city that welcomes us and cuts us down**

nuestras cuevas respectivas   **our respective caves**   rascacielos y caimanes **skyscrapers and alligators**   mangle con mangle   **mangrove meeting mangrove**   sudor con sudor   **sweat meeting sweat**   sudar o dar su huida **to perspire or to retire**   para volver al lugar   **and to return to the place** desde donde se dice que el cielo   **where they say that the sky**   es el lugar que me legas   **is the wreath you bequeath me**   el lugar que te fue llamando hacia mí   **the place that began calling you to me**   a fines del segundo día   **at the end of the second day**   cuando asentiste   **when you nodded** cuando burlaste a la máquina   **when you bypassed the machine**   cuando entendiste que me iba   **when you understood I was leaving**   solo por eso **just for that reason**   para tú quedarte   **for you to stay**   hasta que otro cielo te llamara   **until another sky might claim you**   tal vez el tuyo católico de la duda sabia   **perhaps your catholic sky with its wise doubt**   o tal vez el mío imposible pero bebible entre nubes   **or my impossible sky with its swig of clouds**   como el bilis graffitiado de mi ciudad perdida   **like the graffitied bile of my lost city**   donde una vez estuvimos juntos   **where we were together once**   festejando la posteridad del signo   **celebrating the posterity of the sign**   con ese humor nuestro   **with that silliness of ours**   en el tope del bus   **on a double-decker bus**

turistas por fin   **we're tourists finally**   de los que están claros   **the clear-headed kind**   de los que tiran sus binoculares al río   **that cast their binoculars into the river**   para pescar algo dientudo   **to catch something toothy**   colmilludo   **fanged**   que parece reírse con nosotros   **that seems to be laughing with us**   mientras cruzamos Times Square   **while we cross Times Square**   felices en la cursilería del cuerpo   **happy in the corniness of**

our bodies   sin más ansiedad que la muerte de siempre   **our only anxiety the
same old death**   la que no nos toca todavía   **the one that isn't calling for us
yet**   la de todos los poemas   **the one from all the poems**   la de tu filosofía
the one from your philosophy   la que no conoce ley   **the one that knows
no law**   y por eso nos iremos   **and that's why we'll leave**   desde la muerte
nos veremos por encima del cielo   **from death we'll see each other above
the sky**   nos convertiremos en promontorio   **we'll become a promontory**
sin bandera por fin   **without a flag for once**   solo lo viejo y pellejudo   **with
only the years and the skin and bones**   que hemos vivido juntos o solos
we have lived through together or alone   y tal vez nombrado   **and
perhaps named**   en lo ensombrecido de la tarde   **in the shade of a stifling**
asfixiante y sin brisa   **and airless afternoon**   en que te dejas llamar   **when
you let your name be called**

las enfermeras sí se llamaban   **the nurses' names**   como tú nos contaste
were in fact what you said they were   mujeres como tú   **women like you**
oscuras en lo rojizo y rollizo de tu ciudad   **dark in your ruddy and fleshy city**
tan lejos de la mía   **so far away from mine**   era época de elecciones   **it was
election time**   y los doctores   **and the doctors**   hombres blancos todos
white men all of them   hablaban de migrantes y de acentos   **were talking
about immigrants and accents**   y yo pensaba en el tuyo   **and I thought of
yours**   en cómo nombrabas tu diferencia cada día   **of how you named your
difference every day**   y en la esperanza de que volvieras a hacerlo   **and
of the chance that you might do so once again**   los guardaespaldas del
milagro reían tus gracias   **the miracle's bodyguards had laughed at your
jokes**   permitiéndote acercarte a la luz inalámbrica de la entraña   **allowing
you to gravitate toward the cordless light within**

somos todos el acento   **each one of us is the accent**   con que se dice la palabra
silente   **with which we say the silent word**   somos haches intermedias   **we're
the mute h's**   entre el *ache*-dolor del inglés   **between the English *ache***   y el
aché-santero   **and Santería's *aché***   y es que entre las palabras   **and it's just**

that between words   está el silencio   **there is a silence**   el acento   **an accent**   la relación   **a relation**   lo demás es herramienta   **the rest is a tool** fantasía de irrupción   **a breakthrough fantasy**

a la semana la palabra irrumpe   **a week later a word breaks through**   entre el rumor de las máquinas   **the murmur of machines**   hablas sin entender ni recordar   **you speak not understanding or remembering**   el hemisferio ahora   **the hemisphere now**   es tu jardín dañado   **is your damaged garden**   mis epilepsias   **my epilepsies**   tus infartos   **your strokes**   "lo convulsivo de estar vivo"   **"convulsively alive"**   dirían las pancartas   **the placards would say**   si las hubiera pero no las hay   **if there were any but there aren't**   quedan solo nuestros cuerpos-silencios   **what's left is our bodies-silences**   nuestro dilo-en-sigilo   **our say-it-in-secret**   garganta de arena en la playa prohibida   **throat of sand on the forbidden beach**   con sus fortificaciones de la era colonial   **with its colonial-era fortifications**   de donde vienen nuestros antepasados   **where our ancestors come from** reales y ficticios   **both real and fictitious**

tú tratando de llegarle al pasamanos   **you're trying to reach the handrail** de rehabilitarte   **to rehabilitate yourself**   de habitar un cuerpo   **to inhabit a body**   como si se pudiera   **as if one could**   como si lo que nos tocara **as if that were in the cards**   no fuera asomarnos   **as if our job weren't showing up**   y tomar fotos con teléfonos rotos   **and taking pictures with broken phones**   para difundirlas por las redes   **to post them on networks** donde ya no hay ruido   **by now devoid of noise**   a alguien le gusta **somebody likes it**   otro comenta   **somebody else comments**   con muy pocos caracteres   **using very few characters**

esos son los placeres de comunicarse   **those are the pleasures of communicating**   en este nuevo hemisferio   **in this new hemisphere** donde te canté los Beatles   **where I sang you the Beatles out of tune** desafinando y con el teléfono por fin guardado   **with my phone finally in my**

pocket tratando de guardarte en la memoria **trying to freeze you in a memory** que me es externa **that is external to me** al menos por ahora **at least for now** de atesorarte de frente al terror **to treasure you amid the terror** de ver la cortina **to see the curtain** convertirse en cárcel de barrotes florales **become a jail whose bars blossom**

todos somos avatares de flores **we are all avatars of flowers** en las redes **in the nets where I search for you** donde te busco y te encuentro **and find you** pero sé que no eres tú **but I know that it's not you** porque tú te quedaste en aquella habitación **because you're still in that room** y yo también **and I am too** ahora lo que nos toca es sucesión de renaceres **now we're in line for a series of rebirths** el miedo triunfal de vivir **for the triumphant fear that is being alive** con la boca abierta y llena de arena **with a mouth wide open and full of sand** caracoles en la orilla del tiempo **seashells at the edge of time** donde flotamos sin cuerpo **where we float disembodied** hasta reconocernos **and slow to recognize**

THE GRAND CONQUERORS / EL GRAN CONCURSO

"Grand Concourse Neighborhood
in the South Bronx Gentrifies"

New York Times, March 26, 2012

in search of a grand conquest

a banker that seeks a canker

a tanker that seeks a bunker

a tourist that seeks a stadium

a mayor that seeks a podium

a broker that seeks a break

a realtor that seeks a reject

a rapper that seeks a rep

an activist that seeks a project

a professor that seeks a confessor

a queer that seeks a body

a poet that seeks a people

a blog that seeks an angle

a city that seeks a language

a music that seeks an image

a future that seeks a past

a migrant that seeks a hydrant

a hustler that seeks a haunt

a painter that seeks a method

a family that seeks a clearance

a flyer that seeks a current

a discourse that seeks an audience

a resource that seeks a recourse

a syllable that seeks a song

en busca del gran concurso

banquero que busca su cuero

turista que busca su estadio

alcalde que busca su apoyo

rapero que busca su estilo

activista que busca su proyecto

profesor que busca su confesor

decadente que busca su gente

poeta que busca su pueblo

blog que busca su enfoque

fuerza que busca su choque

ciudad que busca su lenguaje

concursante que busca su premio

curso que busca su rumbo

discurso que busca su audiencia

ciencia que busca su recurso

cursiva que busca su sílaba

excursión que busca su mapa

concreto que busca su decreto

cántico que busca su trópico

cráter que busca su cuerpo

cráneo que busca su carne

cadáver que busca su ave

carretera que busca su palmera

a squirrel that seeks a posse

a rat that seeks a pack

a hairline that seeks an extension

a deco that seeks an art

a novelist that seeks a prize

a canticle that seeks a tropic

a crater that seeks a river

a cranium that seeks a fulcrum

a cubicle that seeks a cloud

a corpse that seeks a course

a boulevard that seeks a palm tree

a construction that seeks a scaffold

a flaneur that seeks a beat

a caravan that seeks an eternity

a diaspora that seeks a flag

a household that seeks its food

a T-shirt that seeks its bones

a skull that seeks its smile

a burning that seeks its morning

a chemistry that seeks its formula

a codex that seeks its apex

a continent that seeks its comrades

a comrade that seeks a camera

a caliphate that seeks a sky

a crisis that seeks its crossings

a comic book that seeks its ending

an excursion that seeks its map

a chronicle that seeks its secret

construcción que busca su andamio

caminante que busca su ritmo

comarca que busca su trasero

charco que busca su barco

calabozo que busca su gozo

descalzo que busca su playa

disco que busca su agujero

ojo que busca su cara

caja que busca su perno

catálogo que busca su prólogo

caravana que busca su eterno

recodo que busca su código

caduco que busca su truco

califato que busca su cielo

comercio que busca su comida

caparazón que busca su palabra

calavera que busca su sonrisa

camisa que busca sus huesos

quemazón que busca su asombro

química que busca su fórmula

capataz que busca su paz

códice que busca su ápice

camarada que busca su cámara

continente que busca sus retazos

cruzacalles que busca su calle

comedia que busca su final

crónica que busca su secreto

SIGNS OF THE HEMISPHERE / LETREROS DEL HEMISFERIO

(signs as seen from a bus, New York City to Albany, 2011)   TAGS AVAILABLE
REDUCE SPEED   SERVICE AREA   VINCE LOMBARDI $AVE MONEY   GEICO
GET LOST   RIO   FORT LEE   GEORGE WASHINGTON   HACKENSACK
PATERSON   HAMPTON INN   CHALLENGER ROAD   LOEWS THEATER
SAMSUNG   AVAILABLE LAND   NO TURNS   KEEP RIGHT   LEONIA   TEANECK
EXPRESS   NORTHRAMP   YOUR SPEED   WELCOME TO HACKENSACK
RAINBOW CLEANERS   QUEEN ANNE THEATRE   LITTLE FERRY   LUKOIL   NO
TRUCKS   MORE FUN   IS MORE FUN   MT. AIRY   SWIFT   AT&T COVERS 97%
PERCENT OF AMERICANS   WOW!

hear me out   human   as I rise from the hum   the humor and rumor
of my tongue   emerging from the humid asphalt   the rumor is my home   as
resin and as residence   where resistance is fragile   and resonance is tactile

I'm missing the tongues of the tribe   so I transcribe   for ages I have
foraged   have rummaged   across these rum-soaked isles   my hum   not
ready for a ream yet   finding its rhythm

I'm hawing hemispheres   in the farthest latitudes   for the hymn
of global mouths forgotten   in its place the loose hem   the stratagem of hum
ahem   I've come to babble   until neurons unravel   glyphs in stereo   no
remedy in standing   nonnative to this soil   this rock   this ruin of focus
groups

remains of a village   sheets of foliage   silence on both sides   wind
quadrants   my landlocked legs   my mind lags and follows   crossing to look
an outlet to the eye

cloud and rustle   rust against moon   the crudest gestures   tossed
in a field   mine   a wakeful subject   decomposing   against windows
means of perception?   meaning is notation   dismal organismal   the logic
of slog   survived by self   I seek how radiance is written   rid of scrawl   no
screened-in radius   all signs are glyphic   open to the touch   survived in song

no head   just nerve   or I die coming down   with the illness of
stillness   mine is the grime   of rhyme unwashed   sediment   markings on
the body   my song sounds like serration   but can it cut this loss?

THE CONTAINER STORE   ANNUAL SALE   CLEAR CHANNEL   RESTAURANT
DEPOT   TENSION ENVELOPES   FLOOR COVERING   LIQUIDATIONS   MAHWAH
HONDA   PARTY BOX   ROCK-BOTTOM PRICES   HOME DEPOT   FIX YOUR
COMPUTER $19.99   INDOOR GO-KARTING   DEERE   BRIDGE FREEZES
ACTION RUBBER   EXXON   OUTBACK   EASTER SEALS   PARK AVE BMW
ENTERING BORO OF PARAMUS   AUTO BODY COLLISION SPECIALISTS   PET
SMART   STAPLES   IKEA DRIVE   LOSE WEIGHT   PLASTIC SURGEON   PET
AMERICA   OPEN MRI   GOLF GALAXY   SUBURBAN DINER   DICK'S   PARAMUS
TOWN SQUARE   CASH 4 GOLD   COURTYARD MARRIOTT   BIJOU BRIDAL
TRADER JOE'S   PETCO   CASUAL MALE   BOB'S FURNITURE   BAGELS AND DELI
SPORTS AUTHORITY

*(letreiros, ônibus, Rio de Janeiro a São Paulo, 2009)   MONTEC CALDEIRARIA E
MONTAGEM   INDUSLAR LAVANDERIAS   GRAAL PNEUS   EMBAIXADOR   E GANHE
UM PÃO SEMOLINA   MOTOVEREDA   COMUNIDADE EVANGÉLICA PROJETO VIDA
BEBA SAÚDE   ÁGUA MINERAL ATTIVA   FURNAS   HOTEL FAZENDA VILLA FORTE*

heme aquí   y que humano   surgiendo del humo   del humor del rumor
que es mi lengua   el húmedo asfalto no me falta   pero el rumor es mi hogar
mi resina y residencia   donde la resistencia es frágil   y la resonancia es táctil

me faltan las lenguas de la tribu   y pues transcribo   forrajeando   de
nombre en nombre   en estas islas de herrumbre   mi reuma   aún busca su
resma   su ritmo

me río en la avería de hemisferio   en las lejanas latitudes   olvidando
el himno   de la roca planetaria   y en su lugar hallo el ruedo suelto   la
estratagema del rumor   en flor   he venido a balbucear   hasta ver el deshilar de
las neuronas   glifos estereofónicos   yo de pie y sin remedio   forastero en este
suelo   esta piedra   esta ruina de relacionistas públicos

remanentes de la aldea   hojas sin plantas   el silencio se quebranta
cuadrantes de viento   mi caminar sin costa   mi mente sin riposta   cruza para
ver   escaparate al ojo

nube sin ave   moho de luna   el crudo ademán   del que duerme
en campo abierto   sujeto despierto   descomponiéndose   sin ventanales
percepciones especulares   mi noción es notación   de animal abismal   la lógica
del lodazal   donde el yo se llora   busco el escrito radiante que aflora   más
allá del garabato   pantalla sin retrato   los letreros ilegibles   pero tocables   se
convierten en tonadas

decapitado   soy nervio   que morirá al final   del mal de la quietud
mío es el limo de la rima sucia   sedimento   el cuerpo y sus marcas   mi canción
chueca aún abarca   aborda la pérdida

*LANCHONETE PARADA OBRIGATÓRIA   INDÚSTRIAS NUCLEARES DO BRASIL   REI
DAS TRUTAS   ANTES DE CONSTRUIR   A 10 KM   BEMVINDO A RIO DE JANEIRO
ENGEMIX   FISCALIZAÇÃO   MANTENHA DISTÂNCIA LONGO TRECHO EM DECLIVE
ALIMENTO   USINA DE ABASTO   CERÂMICA ARTÍSTICA   A 800 M
FERLES INDUSTRIAL   TYREX   SERRARIA E MADEIRERIA   BORRACHARIA AQUI
TRANSPORTES YAKULT   O MELHOR NEGÓCIO ESTÁ AQUI*

the crime of rhyme   whatever stands for breath   just making
room   rheum in the void   making a number of hum-worthy sounds   limning
the sum of nerve and muscle   these skeletons are learning the skill of slow
dissolve   against mortar   they watch blood trickle behind the scenes   fiscal
transfusions   the making of a holding pattern   and behind the pattern   the
jittery jimmying of keys   handheld or digital

these skeletons seek out ablution   solitary on buses   their fate easy
to hum   they are going down together   with the kleptocrats and plutocrats
and technocrats and autocrats   and don't forget the sewer rats   these
skeletons stand in   for the wordless many   the televised nationals of frenzy
who occupy this unserviceable sector

my hum and its avatars   floes and moraines   oceans and outlets
death topographies   where dust is just another powder   cut and ingested
off of unpaid credit cards   no limit   now is when bleat and signal meet
wireless in alleys   the dump truck was here   removing the spyware from
the panopticon   my hum is a log on the side of the road   no log on   no
dialog box   my hum confronts death   embodies its echo   but bypasses its
hectares full of plastic-flower terrariums   and the daily tedium of its shuttered
empowerment zones

a coughless hacking can be heard   over the rooftops in the outlying
areas   listen to the power drills' arias   mock phonic and surrounded by grass
and granite   grin and bear the animus of scaffoldings   the cascading traffic
farawayward masses fading   there is one light and another light   and another
and another   seriality of bulbs and burbs   shots of self in bedroom cams
in urban encampments

my hum still somehow stunned by language   like Langston   smiling
in the cams and jams of midtowns   their ethnic enclaves   carpeted and
marked up and then abandoned   my hum of off bodies in an on planet   an
oración   in corpse orated   against corporate ration   and all reason of nation
where what starts as hum   so soon fades into buzz

VILLA NEGÓCIOS   LOGÍSTICA E TRANSPORTE   LORENPET   EMBALAGENS
FLEXÍVEIS   AUTO ELÉCTRICA   BOMBAS INJETORAS   BAR DA LADEIRA
IMPRESSÃO DIGITAL   PNEUS   BIEMME   O BRILHO   TRUCK   PROMOÇÃO
VENDINHA   NEM DE SÁ   66   DELÍCIA   PINTADA NA BRASA   DO CHASSI
POSTO SOBERANO   EMBREVALE   VOLVO   TOLDOS VITÓRIA   MOTEL KARIMBÓ

el crimen de la rima   nace del aliento   halla su asiento   en la reuma
del vacío   haciendo ruidos rumorosos   bordeando el músculo y el nervio   los
esqueletos aprenden a disolverse lentamente   contra el mortero   ven en tarima
el fluido mortuorio de transfusiones fiscales   los patrones iguales   y detrás del
patrón   el tecleo ebrio de la mano digital

esos esqueletos buscan bautismo   solos en los autobuses   con su
destino tarareable   descienden juntos   junto con los cleptócratas y plutócratas y
tecnócratas y autócratas   y no te olvides de las ratas   esqueletos de rascacielos
que ocupan el lugar   de las masas silentes   ciudadanos del frenesí televisado
ocupando el sector público inservible

los rumores y sus avatares   balnearios y estuarios   océanos y
escenarios   topografías de muerte   donde la polvareda es apenas otro polvo
repartido y olido en tarjetas de crédito   sin pagar o sin límite   ahora se funden
la señal y el son sordo   en callejones inalámbricos   el camión de basura acaba
de pasar   quitándole el spyware al panóptico   mi murmullo es un madero en el
camino   sin palabra secreta   ni número de usuario   mi rumor se enfrenta a la
muerte a diario   reconoce su eco   pero bordea el jardín de flores plásticas   y el
tedio cotidiano de las obras públicas sin acabar

una tos seca se multiplica   sobre las techumbres de los suburbios
escuchad la sinfonía de taladros cómico-fónicos   rodeados de grama y de
granito   soségate y brega con la violencia de los andamios   el tráfico atrófico
paradistantes   las masas pasan y se pierden   queda una luz y otra luz   y otra
y otra   bombillas de vecindarios en serie   autorretratos con web cams de camas
sin sutra   en campamentos urbanos

mi rumor todavía   lenguatónito   como Langston Hughes   sonriendo
en las cámaras de ciudades en tránsito   en sus enclaves étnicos   allanados y
acicalados y luego abandonados   mi rumor de cuerpo puerco en un planeta parco
un blues orado de cuerpo horadado   ante la ración corporativa   y la razón de la
nación   donde el murmullo   deviene barullo

ÁLCOOL   CHEVROLET   SÍTIO DO JUCA   POSTO DE MOLAS GUARÁ   TENDA
ATACADO   SOL AMERICANO   SEM NOIVOS   RENT-A-CAR   JÚLIO TORNEIRO
ATACADISTA   24 HORAS   CHEGUE BEM   EMBAIXADA DO MORRO   CLÍNICA
VETERINÁRIA WAACK   MARIA ELENA CAMARGO   LANCHONETE ENCANTADO
ASSEMBLEIA DE DEUS MADUREIRA

mine's the hum of hemisphere   the silence of its midnight boulevards
from the Bronx's Grand Concourse   to 9 de Julio in Buenos Aires   but not
the paramodern city aping Paris   a modernity of imitation unto parody and
imported Pierrots   and not quite the boulevards of revolution   of blow darts
aimed at the pates of robber barons   instead mine is the hum of Césaire's
archipelagos   and Damas's tam-tams   and Haroldo's galaxies   and Vallejo's
deserts   and Neruda's elements   and Bishop's loping song   and Williams's
blinding island sky   and Martí's angst   and Whitman's wonder   and Paz's
mire   and Sousândrade's vertigo   and Sor Juana's blaze   and the drum's
cry   and the Cree and the Creoles   claiming no decree   but in deictics   all
pointing the way   this way to the Americas by night   its smiling villages and
radiant exurbs   for once at once awake   startled by the hum

no Che in this noche   avoid Evita   no motorcycle in these diaries
don't bother guessing this loco's motive   this loca's stride   the globe's
refraction in drive-thru windows   workers of the world   take off your paper
hats   avoid the avalanche of billboards   own your memory of ocean and of
mountain   the likable catastrophe of your dark eyes   the strophes and stanzas
of your struggle   that shames the wind chimes tired of hanging   yours is the
hum of becoming   refuse the fuselage on fire   the carillon's carrion   the
staging devices and gaming devices   recover the signal in mute emission   the
knottedness of people   no longer pandering to états   your hum defying the
small America   its Anglo angles   and all its inexecutable orders

even without attributes   we are still tribulators   our fate always in
play   our bodies bound by the spray   of bullets and ocean   migrants with
no return policy   always crossing   a bridge without a causeway   corrupting
the program   spiking the punchbowl so it leaks again   this time for good
until the punch cards are full of dances   a neural mass   no longer misfiring
wide-eyed in wartime cities

VENHA CONHECER   NA BASÍLICA   LAR DE DOENTE   USE FAZ   MC DONALD'S
HAMBURGERS   ABASTEÇA AQUI   VOCÊ ESTÁ EM CAMINHO   ANJOS   OBRA DO
GOVERNO DO ESTADO   BAR   LANCHONETE DA CRIS   FAZENDA SÃO FRANCISCO
DA BELA VISTA   PRA CAMIONHEIROS   PINGA   PAVI DO BRASIL   ELMA CHIPS
SUPERFECTA   VENDEDOR   SERRALHERIA VALÉRIO

mío el rumor de hemisferio   el silencio noctámbulo de bulevares   de
la 9 de Julio en Buenos Aires   al Grand Concourse del Bronx   pero no la ciudad
paramoderna de poses en pos de París   una modernidad imitativa hasta la parodia
y sus Pierrots importados   y no del todo los bulevares de revoluciones   de
vanguardias indígenas   apuntando sus saetas hacia las calvas de los mercenarios
el mío es el rumor de los archipiélagos de Césaire   de los tam-tams de Damas
de las galaxias de Haroldo   de los desiertos de Vallejo   los elementos de Neruda
la canción nómada de Bishop   el cielo ciego e isleño de Williams   la angustia
de Martí   el asombro de Whitman   el limo de Paz   el vértigo de Sousândrade
el resplandor de Sor Juana   el clamor en flor de un tambor   la ciudad letrada
hecha letreros   que iluminan las noches americanas   sus villorrios sonrientes
y urbanizaciones radiantes   por fin por ahora despiertos   sorprendidos por el
rumor

esta noche no Che   evita a Evita   no hay motocicleta en estos diarios
no detendrás mi moción de loco   mi nación (dis) loca la refracción del globo
en ventanas de servicarro   obreros del mundo   quítense sus gorros de papel
esquiven la avalancha de cruzacalles   guarden su memoria de océano y montaña
la tierna catástrofe de sus hermosos y oscuros ojos   las coplas y estrofas de su
lucha   que avergüenza a los móviles cansados de reguindar   suyo es el rumor
de un devenir   rechacemos el fuselaje en llamas   la carroña del carillón   los
controles remotos del escenario   recuperemos la emisión muda de la señal   el
nudo de pueblos   ya no en función de estado   ese murmullo suyo desafía a la
pequeña América   la de los ángulos anglo y las órdenes inejecutables

aun sin atributos   somos aún tribuladores   nuestro destino siempre en
juego   nuestros cuerpos en la espuma   de balas y de océano   emigrantes sin
vuelta   siempre cruzando   un puente sin carretera   corrompiendo el programa
envenenando la champán hasta que llueva de nuevo   esta vez a cántaros   y que
el cántaro conlleve el canto y su bailoteo   la masa neural   ya no dispara en falso
por fin despertando en las ciudades en guerra

RETIFICA RODAGEM   DURALAJE   CASA DO FIGUEIRO   CLASSIC CARS
DURATEX   ALINHAMENTO DE DIREÇÃO   USINAGEM   VENDO E ALUGO   VISÃO
ÓCULOS   WENZEL   CANTINA DO MINEIRO   MAXI LAJES   JÚLIO SIMÕES
PROJESUL   PORTAS E JANELAS DE ALUMÍNIO

RIP VAN WINKLE   AMERICAN CANDLE CO   DETROIT DIESEL   INDOOR POOL
WI-FI   EXTRA SPACE STORAGE   DELI PIZZA   FALLEN   ATLAS VAN LINES
SELF-SERVE   HEADLIGHTS   WIPERS   MORE GORE   CAVERNS   CAMP   GO
UNDERGROUND   SCHOOL HOUSE RD   JIMMY'S JUNK   AUTO WRECKING
KAATERSKILL   CAIRO   INDIAN RIDGE   AMERICAN MUSEUM OF FIREFIGHTING
MOBIL   HOME DEPOT   CEVA FREIGHT   GARDEN STATE   CAUTION WIDE
FAMOUS FAMIGLIA   NO BULL   COXSACKIE   RAVENA   NEED THE BEST SEATS?

            seen through your eyes   I see at last   the outlines of the hemisphere
I find my hum in harmony with you   that is   in dissonance with self   in
shared discord   in a storm front shared   and so I name my condition of
islandness   the tropics of trauma that birthed me   my body damaged and
unmanaged   identity in bio-rhythm   labor of movement   in unusual time
signatures   sing timeless tuneless melodiatribe   aimless in meander   out
to the jetty   beyond the observation deck   beyond the tourists in knee-high
gray gym socks   congregating outside gated communities   to take digital
footage of the wreckage they can't see   they cannot hear the hum over their
headphones   the hum of the trade winds on the blood-warm seas   the hum
that hides in our black sand   in our brown skin and our purple sky

            the rattle of bones after the jackhammers   I hear it   the hum of last
resort   the architecture of our capitals   the buzz of our occipitals   the sad
beauty of this claptrap synapse   who hears what I'm reciting?   here's what I'm
resiting   the echo and the wave's crest   I leave the rest to resigning politicians
and the bankers who are gasping for heirs   and so I leave the word in hopeful
ruin   I transcribe our reunion   with your help I begin to transcribe   I
transscrub   I transscrawl   I transcry   while holding ground over the missing
tongue   with your help I begin   I'm reciting the cyst   I'm resisting the sigh
I'm restoring the song   with your help   I'm resetting the sky

GIVE A LAPTOP   BOAT-N-RV   BANQUET HALL   CERTIFIED SCALES   TRAVEL
MART PLAZA   SERVICE AREA RAMP   STOP DWI   ARCTIC ADVENTURES
MASS TPKE   BOSTON   BUFFALO KEEP   29 ACRES   CLEANING SERVICES
TRAVEL INFO   CAPITAL REGION   WELCOME   ERIE CANALWAY   TIMES
UNION   NATIONAL HERITAGE   THRUWAY   CORRIDOR   GROOVED PAVEMENT
VETERANS MEMORIAL   BANKING WITH A PURPOSE   THE PASSION CUT   BOXES
HITCHES   SELF STORAGE   HUDSON RIVER   PORT   ESTUARY   BROADWAY
RAIL STATION   EMPIRE PLAZA   BUSINESS DISTRICT   DUNKIN DONUTS
HOME OF YANKEE DOODLE

viendo por tus ojos   veo por fin   los trazos de hemisferio   hallo
mi tonada en tu armonía   es decir   en el yo disonante   en la discordia
compartida   en la tormenta compartible   y pues nombro mi condición de
isla   el trauma de trópicos que me dio a luz   mi cuerpo dañado y malversado
identidad biorrítmica   la labor del movimiento   fuera de tiempo y de tono
entono la melodiatriba   vueltas sin rumbo   hacia el malecón   más allá del
observatorio   más allá de los turistas en calcetines grises   reunidos a las afueras
de urbanizaciones cerradas   tomando fotos digitales de la ruina que no logran ver
no escuchan el rumor con sus audífonos puestos   el rumor de los vientos alisios
en la sangre caliente del mar   el rumor escondido en nuestra arena negra   en
nuestra piel oscura y nuestro cielo morado

el cascabel de huesos después de los taladros   lo oigo   el rumor sin
más remedio   la arquitectura de nuestras capitales   el zumbido de nuestros
occipitales   la belleza triste de esta astrosa sinapsis   ¿quién escucha lo que
recito?   he aquí lo que repito   el eco y la ola que rompe   el resto se lo
dejo a los políticos que renuncian   a los banqueros que repugnan en busca de
herederos   y pues le cedo mi palabra a la ruina alentadora   y transcribo nuestra
reunión   con tu ayuda comienzo a transcribir   a transgrabar   a transtrepar   a
transclamar   pisando tierra sobre la lengua ausente   con tu ayuda empiezo   a
recitar el tropiezo   a resistir el duelo   a restaurar el canto   con tu ayuda voy
a reiniciar el cielo

GROW DOT-COM TECHNOLOGIES ENHANCE GEO-PROCESSING APPLICATIONS DEPLOY REAL-TIME FUNCTIONALITIES E-ENABLE SEXY DELIVERABLES TRANSFORM SYNERGISTIC SOLUTIONS ITERATE VIRAL COMMUNITIES LEVERAGE OPEN-SOURCE CONVERGENCE INTEGRATE KILLER METHODOLOGIES EXPLOIT IMPACTFUL WEB-READINESS SEIZE DYNAMIC MARKETS ENVISIONEER VISIONARY SYSTEMS TRANSITION UBIQUITOUS E-COMMERCE REVISIT BRICKS-AND-CLICKS CONSUMERS TARGET COMPELLING MODELS ARCHITECT INNOVATIVE SYNERGIES MAXIMIZE CUTTING-EDGE L-SERVICES MESH MAGNETIC PROGRAMS CULTIVATE MOBILE AND WIRELESS APPLICATIONS TARGET ENTERPRISE COMMUNITIES EMBRACE INTUITIVE DELIVERABLES EXPEDITE OUT-OF-THE-BOX COMMUNITIES WHITEBOARD EFFICIENT E-BUSINESS UTILIZE COLLABORATIVE CONVERGENCE EXTEND PLUG-AND-PLAY E-TAILERS STREAMLINE BRICKS-AND-CLICKS SCHEMAS REINTERMEDIATE ONE-TO-ONE FUNCTIONALITIES IMPLEMENT GRANULAR MARKETS MAXIMIZE SEAMLESS INTERFACES REVISIT BRICKS-AND-CLICKS RELATED INTEROPERABILITY OPTIMIZE LOCATION-AWARE METRICS ITERATE REVOLUTIONARY INITIATIVES DISINTERMEDIATE INTEGRATED L-MARKETS REINTERMEDIATE KILLER INFOMEDIARIES BENCHMARK IMPACTFUL CONVERGENCE MONETIZE EXTENSIBLE MARKETS REINVENT USER-CENTRIC E-MARKETS MESH SEXY INFRASTRUCTURES ENGINEER END-TO-END BANDWIDTH E-ENABLE DOT-COM INITIATIVES INCENTIVIZE GEOGRAPHIC PARTNERSHIPS EXPEDITE OUT-OF-THE-BOX MODELS TRANSFORM SEAMLESS METHODOLOGIES ARCHITECT WORLD-CLASS PROGRAMS GROW VERTICAL CONVERGENCE SYNDICATE OPEN-SOURCE RELATIONSHIPS SEIZE CROSS-PLATFORM E-BUSINESS ENHANCE EXTENSIBLE MARKETS TARGET WORLD-CLASS INFRASTRUCTURES GENERATE LOCATION-BASED WEB-READINESS CULTIVATE ONE-TO-ONE NETWORKS LEVERAGE FRICTIONLESS WIRELESS INTEGRATE GRANULAR MOBILE UTILIZE DISTRIBUTED E-COMMERCE BRAND KILLER CONVERGENCE DRIVE SCALABLE TECHNOLOGIES ENGINEER DISTRIBUTED FUNCTIONALITIES LEVERAGE INNOVATIVE CONSTRUCTS GROW OPEN-SOURCE INFOMEDIARIES ENHANCE GLOBAL INITIATIVES E-ENABLE CROSS-MEDIA DELIVERABLES BRAND LEADING-EDGE CHANNELS REVOLUTIONIZE KILLER METHODOLOGIES STRATEGIZE CROSS-MEDIA MODELS BRAND WIRELESS MOBILE CHANNELS INTERNATIONAL IDENTITY ANALYST DYNAMIC IMPLEMENTATION ASSISTANT PRINCIPAL RESPONSE SUPERVISOR CHIEF MOBILITY COORDINATOR LEGACY OPTIMIZATION FACILITATOR FUTURE FACTORS ARCHITECT LEGACY IDENTITY STRATEGIST LEGACY MARKETING DEVELOPER FUTURE INFRASTRUCTURE ENGINEER DYNAMIC DIVISION DESIGNER DIRECT SOLUTIONS TECHNICIAN DYNAMIC MARKETING ORCHESTRATOR CORPORATE GROUP ANALYST FORWARD COMMUNICATIONS ASSOCIATE CORPORATE OPERATIONS DEVELOPER INVESTOR MARKETS OFFICER PRODUCT FACTORS SUPERVISOR INTERNAL DATA AGENT CHIEF PARADIGM ANALYST PRODUCT PARADIGM CONSULTANT CORPORATE PARADIGM ASSOCIATE DYNAMIC RESEARCH AGENT LEGACY QUALITY DESIGNER PRINCIPAL BRAND FACILITATOR INTERNAL ACCOUNTABILITY SPECIALIST INVESTOR SECURITY ENGINEER CENTRAL METRICS SUPERVISOR FORWARD APPLICATIONS FACILITATOR INTEGRATE EFFICIENT E-COMMERCE ARCHITECT WAP-ENABLED INTEROPERABILITY BRAND INTEGRATED INFRASTRUCTURES HARNESS NEXT-GENERATION L-BUSINESS ENHANCE PLUG-AND-PLAY SUPPLY-CHAINS WHITEBOARD BRICKS-AND-CLICKS CONSTRUCTS STREAMLINE PLUG-AND-PLAY PARTNERSHIPS EMPOWER FRICTIONLESS PARTNERSHIPS REPURPOSE INTUITIVE EXPERIENCES ORCHESTRATE E-BUSINESS PARADIGMS MORPH CLICKS-AND-MORTAR USERS TRANSITION KILLER MARKETS GROW GEO-TARGETED SYSTEMS GENERATE STICKY MODELS REINTERMEDIATE END-TO-END METHODOLOGIES ENGINEER FRONT-END ROI EMBRACE BROAD-BASED E-COMMERCE ITERATE MISSION-CRITICAL DELIVERABLES DISINTERMEDIATE GEOGRAPHIC CONSUMERS REVOLUTIONIZE PROACTIVE E-SERVICES CULTIVATE CUTTING-EDGE MARKETS

ACKNOWLEDGMENTS AND NOTES

Some of these poems first appeared in *80grados*; *Barzakh*; *Corresponding Voices*; *Elective Affinities: Cooperative Anthology of Contemporary U.S. Poetry*; *Fence*; *International Poetry Review*; *Lana Turner: A Journal of Poetry and Opinion*; *Luna Luna*; *MAKE: A Chicago Literary Magazine*; *Mandorla: New Writing from the Americas*; *La Más Bella* (Spain); *The Poetry Project Newsletter*; *Transtierros*; *Upstairs at Duroc* (France); *Voices de la Luna*; *Devouring the Green: Fear of a Human Planet*, edited by Sam Witt and Debra Di Blasi (Seattle: Jaded Ibis Press, 2015); and in "What's in a Nombre? Writing Latin@ Identity in America," a special issue of *phati'tude Literary Magazine* edited by Nancy Mercado. "United States / Estados Unidos" was published as a broadside by the Center for Book Arts. Thank you to all the editors and publishers.

Gracias mil to all those who read, commented on, or otherwise nurtured these pages of poetry: Rosebud Ben-Oni; Daniel Borzutzky; Susan Briante; Kristen Buckles and everyone at the University of Arizona Press; Martha Clippinger; Victor Hernández Cruz; John Alba Cutler; LaTasha N. Nevada Diggs; Kristin Dykstra; Carmen Giménez Smith; MC Hyland; Maricarmen Martínez; Valerie Martínez; Steven V. Pacia, MD; Willie Perdomo; Justin Petropoulos; Nicole Peyrafitte and Pierre Joris; Barbara Jane Reyes; Diana Rico; Roberto Tejada; Rodrigo Toscano; my CantoMundo familia; and all those inadvertently omitted.

Certain poems were composed in English and Spanish simultaneously, while others are performative, experimental, or nonequivalent self-translations. In some cases, the line between translation and original is deliberately blurry.

The alphabet poems in "Alphabet City / Ciudad Alfabeto" were composed with the aid of an online N+7 generator.

"Voz Quebrada / Voice Creaks" is an improvised oral poem recorded on a smartphone while walking along Cripple Creek Road in Tallahassee, Florida. It was later displayed as a text-sound-photo installation at the Museo de Arte Contemporáneo de Puerto Rico, as part of the multimedia poetics series Poetry is Busy (December 2010), curated by Yara Liceaga.

"Décimas del Otro Mundo / Otherworldly Décimas" is a contemporary take on the traditional Spanish décima (ten eight-syllable lines rhyming abbaaccddc) but with an Afro-Taíno refrain.

"Heaves of Storm / Embates de Tormenta" began as a series of smartphone photos and bilingual text notes in response to the University of Puerto Rico student strikes of 2009 to 2010. The title of the poem and the last line of each section are taken from Emily Dickinson's poem "I heard a Fly buzz—when I died—."

"Notebook of a Return to the Native Wall Street" is a mash-up of two long transnational poems of the Americas: it alternates between the opening passage of Aimé Césaire's *Cahier d'un retour au pays natal* (Notebook of a Return to the Native Land, 1939) and the first stanzas of Sousândrade's "O inferno de Wall Street" (Wall Street Inferno), Canto X of his 1870s epic *O Guesa errante: Poema americano* (Wandering Guesa: American Poem). The (mis)translations of the original French and Portuguese were generated by Google Translate.

The Spanish version of "Pastoral" is an improvised oral poem that appeared in slightly different form in my short book *Los días porosos* (Guatemala City: Catafixia Editorial, 2012). It was recorded on a smartphone while walking along Vacía Talega Beach in Puerto Rico (see "Primer día 4:13 p.m." on my YouTube channel urayoannoel).

"United States / Estados Unidos" was almost entirely composed with an anagram generator app for smartphone, as was the last part of "Major Tom (Coming Home)."

"Variaciones Sobre un Paisaje de Violeta López Suria / Variations on a Landscape by Violeta López Suria" was inspired by the Puerto Rican poet Violeta López Suria (1926–94) and especially by the two lines of hers that serve as its epigraph. The text at the bottom of each page is a collage of Internet search engine results (as in Flarf poetry) for the name Violeta López Suria.

"You Have the Nice Weather" is a homophonic translation of Sor Juana Inés de la Cruz's seventeenth-century sonnet "Quéjase de la suerte [. . .]" ("She complains of her lot . . . ," included at the bottom of the page) performed by reading the Spanish original into a smartphone with voice recognition set to English.

The prose blocks of "Scene Apps" are my free-form and selective translations of passages from father of modern neurology Jean-Martin Charcot's book *Les démoniaques dans l'art* (Demoniacs in Art, 1887), a collaboration with anatomist and artist Paul Richer. The word lists in between were generated with a random-word generator app for smartphone and then (mis)translated using Google Translate.

The first part of "Langú" mixes English, Spanish, and Ojibwe (and, in the refrain, Garifuna, Papiamento, and Inupiat). The three alphabet poems that follow are made up of lists of words and phrases in Tupí-Guaraní, Mixtec, and Haitian Kreyòl, respectively, while the English poems below them are my own loose translations/ adaptations of the alphabet poems. All the non-English and non-Spanish text was taken from online dictionaries and databases. This piece was inspired by a whirlwind reading of LaTasha N. Nevada Diggs's book *TwERK*.

The text at the top and bottom of each page of "Signs of the Hemisphere / Letreros del Hemisferio" is a collage of signs seen during two bus rides from Manhattan to Albany, New York, and from Rio de Janeiro to São Paulo, Brazil.

The untitled text at the end of the book was produced by online buzzword and job-title generators.

About the Author

Urayoán Noel is the author of the critical study *In Visible Movement: Nuyorican Poetry from the Sixties to Slam* and several books of poetry in English and Spanish, the most recent of which is *EnUncIAdOr*. Also a performer and translator, he has been a fellow of CantoMundo and the Ford Foundation, and he currently serves as a contributing editor for NACLA. Born in San Juan, Puerto Rico, Noel lives in the Bronx and is an assistant professor of English and Spanish at New York University.